Mile High Miracle

Elway and the Broncos: Super Bowl Champions at Last

by Jerry Green

MASTERS PRESS

A Division of Howard W. Sams & Company

Masters Press (A Division of Howard W. Sams & Co.)
2647 Waterfront Parkway, East Drive, Suite 100
Indianapolis, IN 46214

Library of Congress Cataloging-in-Publication Data

Green, Jerry.
   Mile high miracle : Elway and the Broncos, Super Bowl
champions at last / by Jerry Green.

     p. cm.
   ISBN 1-57028-210-2
   1. Denver Broncos (Football team) -- History. 2. Elway,
John, 1960- . 3. Super Bowl (Football game) I. Title.

  GV956.D37G74   1998
  796.332'64'0978883--dc21   98-13455
                                                CIP

Dedication

In memory of Dick Connor, my Denver friend and colleague.

And to the other eight of us with guts of steel and brains to match who've made it through the first XXXII of these yearly clambakes to enchant America with our prose — Larry Felser, Jerry Izenberg, Dave Klein, Will McDonough, Norm Miller, Bob Oates, Edwin Pope, John Steadman.

Credits

Cover Photos©James V. Biever

Inside Photos©James V. Biever and Vernon Biever

Cover Design by Suzanne Lincoln

Edited by Kim Heusel

Text Layout by Kim Heusel

Table of Contents

Introduction vii

The Crushed Orange 1

To the Victor Go the Spoils 18

Rocky Mountain Low 23

No Time for Mickey Mouse 40

The Fifteen Minutes 45

Even His Name Says TD 64

A Loudmouth Bleeping Linebacker 68

The Avalanche 73

"We Come to Win...Period" 94

The Migraine 99

The Orange Hush 134

Introduction

It occurred to me as I listened to John Elway deliver another enchanting quote to an international gaggle of media marvels — John was adorned in dark plastic wraparound shades lest the California sun emerge — that I had now spent nearly eight months of my life covering XXXII Super Bowls.

Thirty-two weeks in 32 years in a variety of locations as diverse as San Diego, where I stood on this cloudy morning shortly after dawn, to New Orleans, Miami, Phoenix to home in Detroit.

"It was tougher this year," Elway said. "We had to go through Kansas City, we had to go through Pittsburgh.

"We realize it's not just important being here.

"You feel the wrath of a town if you don't win."

Ugh!

Denver again. The Broncos, 0-for-4 in previous Super Bowls. Elway, 0-for-3. The American Football Conference 0 for the past 13 Super Bowls.

Oh!

Elway was perched on a podium with 132 reporters forming a semicircle around him on the sidelines of Qualcomm Stadium, San Diego. A half dozen microphones wrapped in fuzzy ersatz — fur coverings attached to booms poked over the rabble. The metal poles threatened Elway's dental work.

I jotted Elway's pithy remarks into the notebook I use only to chronicle Super Bowls. Bret Favre and the Packers would be out later in the morning, perhaps after the sun arrived.

There was nowhere else I'd rather be.

◆　　◆　　◆

Among the souvenirs collected in pursuit of truth and Super Bowl substance are:

Thirty-two medallions or pins issued by NFL propagandists to press/media to distinguish us from autograph hunters, groupies, camp followers and other jock lovers by the yellow-jacketed NFL security specialists.

Thirty-two Super Bowl game programs.

Thirty-two Super Bowl briefcases, to hold 64 media guides.

Thirty-two official Super Bowl ballpoint pens complete with Super Bowl insignia so that I might take only positive notes in my 32 NFL-issued Super Bowl notebooks.

Thirty-two official Super Bowl patches.

Thirty-two used game credentials. Plus memories of 632 Danish pastries consumed, plus 1,132 chunks of sliced honey dew melon, all supplied by NFL propagandists, while chasing interviews with 64 Super Bowl quarterbacks.

My treasure-lode of memorabilia — called junk by my wife, Nancy — is to be found in various places among my collected rubble of more than three decades.

I never throw anything away.

But strangely, among all this, err, stuff, there is not one official NFL Super Bowl megaphone with Roman numerals on the cone and a portrait of Pete Rozelle. Or Paul Tagliabue.

The simple fact is we the media are not cheerleaders. We are, in essence, hard-boiled, crabbed, cynical men — and now a few women — devoid of empathy. This is the case no matter how much the fans of Denver or the newspaper readers of Detroit or the suffering football followers of Chicago believe we should be up rooting with them for THEIR team.

We are ruled by a code — and it is very, very strict.

NO CHEERING IN THE PRESS BOX.

Of course, the occasional television personality might be adorned in Broncos blue skivvies with splashes of orange. The odd newspaper editor might command his paper to display shrieking WE'LL BEAT 'EM headlines on the front page just when Bill Clinton is fighting off another media blitz.

But among us — the true, blue sporting print journalists of America — except maybe in Denver — there is no rooting at the games we cover.

We are neutral grouches.

So to speak.

So why was it that secretly, in our heart of hearts, on January 25, 1998, at Super Bowl XXXII the majority of us ink-stained wretches were hoping John Elway would win.

Sentimental slobs are we!

The very moment the Green Bay gates were opened and Terrell Davis barged into the end zone and the Denver Broncos went ahead at Super Bowl XXXII there were smirking smiles in the upper regions of Qualcomm Stadium. No cheers. No high-fives. No pumping fists.

Just the satisfaction that a quarterback who had labored through 15 seasons could raise both arms in triumph. At age 37.

As protagonist in three prior Super Bowls, John Elway had endured the grilling of three Media Days. Three thousand journalists from news/entertainment outlets all with agendas as strangely varied as *The Wall Street Journal* and MTV, exercised their First Amendment privileges. They were granted leave to ogle the athletes and ask inane questions. Often the responses were equally as inane.

Following these sessions, Elway had endured more interrogation and inspection for two additional days. His words were translated into Japanese, Dutch, French, Spanish, German and proper English. His meanings were interpreted, challenged, psychoanalyzed. His habits were scrutinized. The candy he gave away to the neighborhood kids on Halloween was regurgitated. His facial expressions and prominent teeth were lampooned. His Super Bowl week activities were detailed and criticized.

This was all before the Super Bowl games. Three times, the same questions, some 1,532 of them. In all three of these ultimate games, Elway suffered as the losing quarterback. He was never ridiculed. But his team was, and his city was. Elway merely became the caricature of a loser, the hugely talented quarterback who failed to win a Super Bowl.

And near the end of the 1997 NFL season, it had appeared he would never get another chance. The Broncos had finished their season in second place in the AFC Western Division. They qualified for the Super Bowl tournament as a wild card, a sneered-at outsider. They had to defeat the Jacksonville Jaguars, the upstart expansionists who had kayoed them the year before. Then they would be forced to defeat the Kansas City Chiefs and Pittsburgh Steelers — away from Denver — in hostile environments.

Such were their accomplishments when they staggered into Super Bowl XXXII — to combat the reigning champions and heavily favored Packers and their Green Bay tradition.

Media Day 1998, at Super Bowl XXXII, occurred on a cold, cloudy morning. Elway, sporting wraparound sunglasses, brought back memories of another Super Bowl quarterback, Jim McMahon. McMahon had worn shades indoors a dozen years earlier. Perhaps, Elway had learned to hide his expressions. The questions were fired, all with the stigma of history attached — all referring to the three Super Bowl losses in his file.

And now the intellegensia of pro football figured Elway would in five days become a four-time loser. He would match Jim Kelly, whose Buffalo Bills flopped in four consecutive Januarys earlier in the 1990s. His career would be stained.

When the Broncos first squeezed into Super Bowl XXXII, the oddsmakers out of Las Vegas had calculated that Elway would feel the wrath of Denver again by 14 points. Those odds had been reduced to 12 points by Media Day, on Tuesday of Super Bowl week, and to 11½ by game time. The Broncos were the third-largest underdogs in the 32 years of the game.

"I'd rather be a 15-point favorite myself," said Elway. He added in a wistful tone: "We've been underdogs every time we've been here."

The words were jotted into the notebook.

Denver's Super Bowl history reached into pre-Elway times. The Broncos had qualified for Super Bowl XII, back in 1978, with Craig Morton as their quarterback. They lost — of course — to the Dallas Cowboys, 27-10, in the Louisiana Superdome.

They reached that game as crabby as the sports journalists. Red Miller, then the coach, said in his attempt to produce harmony in the locker room he had appointed a bitch coach.

It made excellent copy . . . the bitch coach and Lyle Alzado and the Denver fans and the guy who wore the orange barrel held over his vitals by suspenders.

Denver had established an image, a tradition.

The Broncos were the first so-called professional major-league team in Colorado. They were originals in the American Football League when it was founded to challenge the 40-year-old NFL in 1960.

They played football those first years with a gaggle of jokers, outcasts, rejects and circus performers — in clown uniforms. The motif was gold and brown — with stocking stripes that ran up and down. Vertical stripes, a Denver-only football fashion.

Somehow Denver managed to keep the Broncos in those early AFL years of a bitter and costly pro football war. The NFL, led by Pete Rozelle, haughtily referred to the AFL as THE OTHER LEAGUE.

The Other League survived. In 1966, with the AFL dragging away NFL draftees such as Joe Namath and threatening to kidnap NFL quarterbacks, peace was arranged. A manufactured peace, negotiated in a clandestine meeting between the NFL's Tex Schramm and the AFL's Lamar Hunt. They sat in a Buick in the parking lot at Dallas' Love Field. As planes landed and left, they worked out a scheme.

There would be a merger. There would be a game between the champions of the two leagues. Teams from the two leagues would play each other in exhibition games. Other details of the merger would be worked out.

Denver — the one-time minor-league town one mile above sea level — was in the big leagues. Sort of.

The establishment NFLers were grudging in their acceptance. They did not graciously welcome Denver, Kansas City, Oakland, San Diego and the other outposts of the AFL.

The first AFL-NFL World Championship Game was scheduled for January 15, 1967, in the Memorial Coliseum, Los Angeles. Pete Rozelle refused to call it The Super Bowl. Too jazzy for the staid league.

◆ ◆ ◆

Back in Kansas City, Lamar Hunt noticed his young daughter bouncing a hard-shelled rubber ball. The AFL had been Hunt's brainchild. He had formed the Dallas Texans as an AFL original franchise. The Cowboys and NFL soon ran him off into exile in Kansas City, where his team was renamed the Chiefs.

Hunt's daughter bounced the ball and it ricocheted above her head. It was a new-fangled toy, popular with the kids.

"What's that called?" Hunt said.

"It's a super ball," said the little girl.

"Aha," said Hunt. The thought would not vanish from his head.

And so the Super Bowl received its name — Rozelle would acquiesce by the third year — from a popular bouncing toy.

◆　◆　◆

Vince Lombardi symbolized the entire NFL. He coached the Green Bay Packers. They were his creation, they were built in his image. They were precisioned, methodical, effective, dominant.

They won the NFL championship and would represent tradition and history in the first championship game. It would eventually become known as Super Bowl I.

Their opponents were the frisky, outspoken Chiefs, owned by Lamar Hunt and coached by the flamboyant Hank Stram. His team, also, reflected his personality.

The Chiefs boasted and preened. They were billeted in Long Beach. The press descended on their hotel. Stram invited the reporters in, welcoming especially those who had been covering the NFL clubs. For interviews, the journalists were told to visit the Chiefs in their rooms.

Lombardi hid the Packers up the California coast in Santa Barbara. The NFL arranged for busses to transport the writers to the Packers hideaway.

The Press/Media Day zoo had not yet been conceived by the propagandists. The first Super Bowl had attracted less than 350 journalists, insufficient in numbers to create a mob scene.

The two rival leagues had declared peace, but they were still fighting the remnant of their war. Lombardi heightened the mood when he met with the press. If the writers could find Bart Starr or Jim Taylor or others of the famed Packers in the hotel lobby, lucky for them. They all preached Lombardi's doctrine of NFL supremacy.

Green Bay won that first Super Bowl over the Chiefs, 35-10. The Packers dominated and at the conclusion ridiculed the Chiefs.

Lombardi, himself, tried to avoid knocking the other league.

He stood in the Packers' locker room up the Coliseum runway and perhaps a dozen writers forced him into a corner.

Lombardi flipped a football. On the ball was etched the words THE DUKE. It was an NFL ball. In this first one, each team used its own league's familiar football on offense.

"That an NFL ball?" I asked Lombardi. The words THE DUKE were clearly visible. Lombardi didn't answer. The question was posed again. "This is an NFL ball," Lombardi said through his gapped teeth, "and it kicks a little bit better, it throws a little bit better and it catches a little bit better."

Stram, next door, stuck up for the AFL. "I don't think one game is any criterion to decide the strength of two leagues," he said.

Lombardi had more to say: "I don't think Kansas City compares with the top teams in the NFL. Dallas is a better team."

Lombardi looked at us with THE DUKE in his hands.

"There, dammit," he said. "You made me say it. Now I've said it."

I swear I saw a flash of lightning shooting from between the gap in his upper teeth.

In August 1967, I flew on the Detroit Lions' charter plane to Denver. It was my first trip to the city. The Lions would be playing the Broncos in the first exhibition game between the NFL and AFL — the first meeting after the Green Bay conquest of Kansas City in the Super Bowl.

The Lions, themselves, were a proud, snickering group when they reached the AFL city.

"If we don't beat Denver, I'll walk back to Detroit," Alex Karras proclaimed to the press.

His words were transformed into headlines.

Karras was an All-Pro NFL defensive tackle, with a streak of nastiness. Often his words were outrageous. Often he backed up his outrageous statements.

The exhibition game was in the University of Denver Stadium. Early in the game, Denver moved the ball on Detroit. After one hard carry by Cookie Gilchrist, an AFL legend and symbol, Karras kicked one of his cleated football shoes. His aim was excellent, on target. He hit Gilchrist in the helmet. Karras was booted out of the game.

The Broncos scored one for the AFL that night. It was a first exhibition game, but it was historic. The Broncos beat the Lions, 13-7.

When the Lions' charter left Denver around midnight, I was aboard near a fuming Joe Schmidt, the Hall of Fame middle linebacker and new head coach. Karras was seated several rows behind us.

Even so, Colorado newspapers reported that Karras had been seen walking eastward some place in Nebraska — Wahoo, or some place. And his trek was tabulated daily in the press — and read with grins and guffaws.

The Broncos' victory was celebrated throughout the AFL. On another team charter that night, Lance Alworth grabbed the intercom to announce Denver's victory to his teammates on the San Diego Chargers.

◆　　◆　　◆

A bunch of us outlanders from Detroit sat in the Buckhorn Exchange in Denver during the 1996 Stanley Cup playoffs. To be honest, we were rubes. We marveled at Denver's growth into a cosmopolitan city. We cherished the cuisine, the rugged fare that cowboys thrived on when the west was the west.

"Try it," one of us suggested. "Great appetizer before your buffalo steak."

So an order was placed — for mountain oysters.

"What are they?" asked one of our contingent.

This old man, who'd been around enough to be regarded as cosmopolitan, offered the answer.

"Bull's testicles. A delicacy, I've been told."

By this time, Denver, from an AFL upstart in 1960, had grown into a town that played with balls and now a puck in all four of the recognized professional sports. The city had added ice hockey to its sporting diversity.

Very cosmopolitan, indeed.

The Colorado Avalanche were in the process of winning the Stanley Cup as champions of the National Hockey League.

This would be a brand-new experience for Denver. The city had never had the excitement, the bragging rights of a world-championship, major-league team.

And the long-suffering folks of Denver, and all of Colorado and parts of Wyoming and Utah, cheered on and preened over their precious Avalanche. This was championship love.

The dear Avalanche had resided in Denver all of one season when they won the city's first championship. The franchise recently had been the Quebec Nordiques — and when that French-speaking Canadian citadel failed to display sufficient love, it was plucked away by Denver.

In one season, the Avalanche had accomplished for Denver what the Broncos had failed to do in 36 seasons. Plus the Avs had a star that matched the magnitude of John Elway — Patrick Roy.

Denver is passionate about its teams.

In baseball, the Colorado Rockies are adored. Created via expansion, the Rockies were instantly successful as the first major-league baseball team in the Mountain Time Zone. They sold out their games at the Mile High Stadium — with the white, bucking stallion beyond the outfield/end zone — they shared with the Broncos. The Rockies attracted more than 3 million paying customers annually, highest in the majors. Such loyalty merited a new ballpark. Coors Field was built. It was state of the art, with the old-fashioned ballpark feel. The Rockies reached the National League pennant playoffs in their third season of existence.

They were another reason for envy by the Broncos, stuck alone in the old Mile High Stadium.

Plus, the Rockies had a sporting star that matched the magnitude of John Elway — Larry Walker.

The one club the Broncos could sneer at was the Denver Nuggets, the city's NBA club.

As the Broncos were being grilled the days before Super Bowl XXXII, the Nuggets were establishing marks for futility in the NBA. Their record was 2-and-38 for the season, they had a losing streak of 23 games.

Lots of wrath in town.

Then on the eve of Super Bowl XXXII, the Nuggets won — they beat the Los Angeles Clippers up the Coast from San Diego.

The mood was set for a glorious Denver weekend.

◆　　◆　　◆

It's about money. Of course.

Money was the essence back in '66 when the NFL and AFL merged, and the value of Denver's pro football franchise skyrocketed.

The AFL had outbid the NFL for a drawling Pennsylvania lad named Joe Willie Namath, who passed footballs with dazzling effectiveness for Bear Bryant at Alabama. The auction for Namath — between the New York Jets of The Other League and the St. Louis Cardinals of the established pro league — soared into a six figures. Such money had never been flipped around before by the pro football franchise owners.

The Jets won Namath — for $424,000. A few years later Namath would win equality for the AFL clubs by guaranteeing the first Super Bowl victory over an NFL team. It was Super Bowl III. Namath and the Jets were 18-point underdogs to the Baltimore Colts of Don Shula. The Colts were reputed to be invincible.

Between dates with his stable of girl friends, Namath managed to pull off a 16-7 victory.

Pete Rozelle's game plan changed. Rather than maintain two leagues with interlocking schedules and separate identities, with a Super Bowl championship game, it was decided to have one greater NFL. There would be National and American Conferences.

Three NFL franchises — the Colts, Cleveland Browns and Pittsburgh Steelers — would switch to join the AFL teams in the American Conference.

The two television networks that had broadcast the rival leagues — CBS the Nationals and NBC the Americans — would continue to rule. And Rozelle, in his financial wizardry, concocted the idea of a Monday night game each week — and peddled it to ABC.

Money remained the essence through all the seasons. Revenues rose by the mega-million. Ultimately, the six-figure incomes of the athletes, the standard established by Namath, would jump to seven figures. Six, seven million for quarterbacks the ilk of John Elway and Brett Favre. This was the evolution of the business portion of pro football.

The game, itself, would change only a bit. Blocking techniques would be refined; the rules governing pass coverage would be tinkered with; rules protecting the quarterback would be tightened; the goalposts would be picked up and moved from the goal line to the back of the end zone.

Super Bowls would become more and more popular, tickets would become more and more difficult to procure. It cost $6 to $12 to buy a ticket to watch the Chiefs and Packers at Super Bowl I. It would cost 275 bucks for a ticket to watch the Broncos and Packers at Super Bowl XXXII — and scalpers were asking $3,000 for two in San Diego.

Corporations ignored Super Bowl I. The Coliseum was one-third empty — or two-thirds filled, according to the optimism of Pete Rozelle.

And we the media were the not quite 350 strong at Super Bowl I that week in January 1967. We were basically from newspapers, the print medium. Only a few TV reporters had been assigned. Cable television was an idea locked deep inside the brain of Ted Turner. ESPN, CNN, FOX were not yet a gleam in their founders' eyes.

Nine of us writers and six photographers survived through all the decades to reach Super Bowl XXXII with streaks intact. Interview the players in their rooms? Those who dared would be bounced out of the lobbies of the team hotels by the NFL's army of security agents.

We were part of the swarm, the '90s-style feeding frenzy.

The media contingent had exploded to the stampeding 3,000 at Super Bowl XXXII in January 1998. Most of them were TV types, with booms and heavy metal video cams that could slice open scalps, people with sharp elbows and insightful questions for athletes like John Elway: "If you could be a tree, what kind of tree would you want to be?"

I do not fool around. That was an actual Super Bowl Media Day question once upon a time.

But the silliness of the media did not impact the public appeal of the Super Bowl through the ages. Eight Super Bowls rank among the top 15 all-time television ratings according to the famed Nielsen ratings.

The first Super Bowl attracted an apathetic audience. And as part of the merger agreement hammered out by Tex Schramm and Lamar Hunt, it was televised by two networks. The NFL's CBS and the AFL's NBC did it, just as the rival leagues passed and ran with their own friendly footballs.

At Super Bowl XXXII, ESPN with a crew of hundreds, FOX Sports and CNN-SI rigged their own studios along the waterfront in San Diego to present all the pregame analysis and gossip. Old Super Bowl players such as Joe Theismann and Tom Jackson and coaches such as John Madden and Joe Gibbs appeared on camera as expert pontiffs.

It was NBC's turn to telecast the game between the underdog Broncos and ruling champion Packers, with the eloquent Dick Enberg.

Enberg would describe Terrell Davis' run to victory — NBC had been the American's network for more than 32 years. And a few moments later, Enberg would sign off in NBC's final pro football game of a happy and prosperous era. Until the next round of network bidding.

A week or so before the hype and marching for Super Bowl XXXII had started, Paul Tagliabue, the late Rozelle's successor, had completed negotiations for the new TV contracts. NBC lost out. CBS regained a spot in this bit of moveable chairs. FOX, ABC, ESPN, along with CBS, gained the rights to telecast NFL games into the 21st century.

The accumulative price was $17.6 billion.

Jerry Green
Grosse Pointe Woods, Mich.
February 1998

Mile High Miracle

Elway and the Broncos: Super Bowl Champions at Last

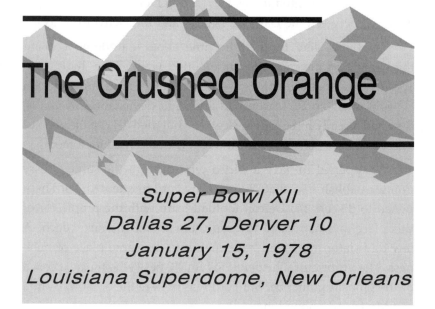

The Crushed Orange

Super Bowl XII
Dallas 27, Denver 10
January 15, 1978
Louisiana Superdome, New Orleans

Free drinks. Free pretzels. Free gossip. The mixture can be deadly. And if the Super Bowl media mob made up the largest collection of freeloaders in the history of mankind, the same group formed the world's largest gaggle of gossipmongers. We fuel on all of this stuff, and the Super Bowl is fertile territory for rumor and speculation.

There are a thousand writers with a thousand ideas elbowing for a tiny bit of something different. We come from every city in the country and cover every club in Pete Rozelle's domain. And the timing is beautiful, the middle of January. All the coaches who are going to be fired have been fired, the final ruins of the previous season. But all the coaches who are going to be hired for the following season have not yet been interviewed, not yet had their brains dissected by discriminating owners who have no concept about the proper way to don a jockstrap.

The result is we stand in Rozelle's press room helping ourselves to NFL refreshments and trying to impress the guys we are swapping rumors with that we are very smart and very well-connected.

1

Such was the situation as I arrived in New Orleans for Super Bowl XII between the Dallas Cowboys and the Denver Broncos.

The Lions were, for the third time, about to undergo a coaching change in the midst of Super Bowl week. They had given Tommy Hudspeth the ziggy — Joe Schmidt's ancient description — right after the '77 season had ended in devastation. Actually, they had already hired his replacement, but tried to keep their choice a secret. For some reason, they thought it would hold for a month.

I happened to have a friend who dealt at the same Grosse Pointe establishment that William Clay Ford frequented. Ford happened to discuss his Detroit football team with the proprietor of this place and happened to drop the name of the next coach. A few days later my friend happened into the same place of business. The proprietor whispered to him: "Guess who the next coach of the Lions is gonna be. Bill Ford was in here the other day and . . . " My friend phoned me.

"Monte Clark's going to coach the Lions," he told me.

"Balderdash," said I.

"Yeah, Bill Ford goes to the same shop as I do and he said it to the guy and the guy told me and I'm telling you, but protect me," said my friend.

"You're a good friend," I said, and fumbled around for a bit, searching for Monte Clark's phone number in the California mountains. I got him on the first ring.

"Where'd you hear that?" Clark said.

"Well, I heard it," I said.

Clark wouldn't confirm that my source was right, but then he didn't say he was wrong, either. We talked about football for a bit, what he'd been doing since he'd been unjustly fired by the San Francisco 49ers. I wrote the story. My paper splashed it across the front page of the news section.

Everybody laughed and said I was dead wrong.

My competition was proclaiming that Chuck Knox, still head coach of the Rams, was going to the Lions. Knox had been an assistant in Detroit under Joe Schmidt and an assistant with the Jets when they won Super Bowl III. He was itching to escape from the Rams and get back to the Lions. He had almost succeeded a year earlier in a plan he masterminded with help from Schmidt, the old coach. Ford wanted Knox at that time and made a hard pitch for him. But Carroll Rosenbloom, who had traded his franchise in Baltimore for the team in Los Angeles, demanded a number of Detroit players to free Knox.

"They're trying to steal my coach," Rosenbloom said.

Now a year later, Rosenbloom was trying to get rid of Knox after the Rams had failed to reach the Super Bowl. He begged the Lions to take him. But Ford had been embarrassed by the Knox affair the previous year. Besides, he had already hired Clark.

None of this had been announced. Talking to Schmidt, I was told Knox was going to Buffalo, where Jim Ringo had been fired. Knox had phoned Ford. Ford refused to take the call. Still, my competition was touting Knox as the next Lions coach.

And Jimmy the Greek went out on CBS with his exclusive prediction: "I have learned that Chuck Knox will be going to the Detroit Lions, and Monte Clark will be the next coach of the Buffalo Bills. My sources are unimpeachable."

At Dallas, two nights before the Cowboys played in the NFC championship game, I encountered the Greek in the pressroom. He walked in with Brent Musburger.

"It's the other way around," I said to them. "Ford won't have Knox. He's already hired Clark. And I've been told Chuck Knox is going to Buffalo."

"You're wrong," said the Greek. "You got it backwards. You're full of it."

Now it was 10 days later, in New Orleans. The Super Bowl media mob stood in the NFL's hospitality room in the new Hyatt Regency. We were drinking the free drinks, munching the free pretzels, exchanging the free gossip. It was the eve of the annual photo day, a Monday evening.

3

"Who you guys gonna believe?" I said, polishing the official Super Bowl XII media pin on my sweater. "Jimmy the Greek or me?"

"You're full of crap," said my friend New York.

We went out to dinner at Arnaud's and then over to the Old Absinthe House. The gossip got deeper and deeper as the night got later.

Tuesday morning, we were off to the Broncos and then the Cowboys. I stood on the field at Tulane in a group talking to Red Miller, the Denver coach. Miller had a face that looked like a broken fist. He was keeping us interested, and when the guy holding the TV camera shoved me, I decided it was time to hold my turf. The TV guys, traveling in triplicate with cameras, sound doohickeys and mikes, were getting thicker and pushier. I was standing there, and they were encroaching. Now a foreign hand had tried to force me back. So I shoved the TV cameraman back. We exchanged a couple of bleep-yous. But fortunately — probably for me — that was the end of it. We both had work to do.

We knew Tom Landry and could predict what he would say all week long. But Miller was somebody new, with new thoughts, as John Madden had been the previous year.

"I'm here for one reason — to help the players play better on Sunday," said Miller. The Broncos had forced Miller's predecessor, John Ralston, out of his job with constant bitching. Lyle Alzado, the bearded terrorist/pass rusher, was ringleader of the mutineers.

"I appointed a bitch coach," said Miller. "It's Randy Gradishar, our linebacker. I want them bitching to improve during the week. If they're not complaining about something, something's wrong.

"The bus driver took a wrong turn and we were on the freeway another 10 minutes. That was a good bitch. We didn't have any grits served at breakfast. Rubin Carter, he wants some grits. He bitched a little. Otis Armstrong found a cockroach in his room. That was real good. Otis did a good job of bitching on that."

Miller had been a heavyweight boxer in his youth, fighting in the Golden Gloves. I should have asked him for a lesson and taken on the TV guy.

◆ ◆ ◆

I wasn't in a great mood on the buslift to the Cowboys' session. We were back at the scene of Duane Thomas' Great Silent Scenario. I glanced at my watch and figured it belonged in Canton, at the Pro Football Hall of Fame.

It was cold and boring. More Tom Landry. Roger Staubach, the square, had become the premier quarterback in football.

The quarterback matchup provided one element of intrigue for those of us desperate for an angle. The Denver quarterback was none other than poor Craig Morton. Staubach versus Morton. A retreat in history, to the Dallas quarterback rivalry after Don Meredith fell for the blandishments of television. You wanted to hold a pity party for Morton. Morton was the Dallas quarterback who threw the ball somewhere toward Dan Reeves and had it intercepted in the waning moments of Super Bowl V. Baltimore kicked the field goal to win that weird football game. Morton was the guy who alternated with Staubach the following year as Landry went bonkers. Tom finally settled on Staubach, a decision of brilliance it turned out, and won Super Bowl VI. Morton had drifted away. Now he had resurfaced in the Super Bowl, on the other side. His old Dallas teammates were overjoyed.

"I think he won't finish the game," said Cliff Harris, who had once failed to scare Lynn Swann out of a Super Bowl.

Harris was a balding safetyman. He looked more like the bartender at the Old Absinthe House than an athlete. He had come out of mighty Ouachita Baptist to become an intimidator in the NFL. He had nearly caused a riot in Super Bowl X when he went clubbing into Roy Gerela. This was the guy Jack Lambert body-flipped to the grass. Now after giving us a geography lesson — Ouachita Baptist could be located in Arkadelphia, Arkansas — Harris was taking a contract out on Morton.

5

"Craig has a bad hip," Harris said. "I think he won't finish the game. Any time you have a guy hurting, he might not finish the game. With him out, it'll be a different game.

"I think anybody can be psyched. That's part of my own philosophy of football. But Craig knows me. He might be less prone to being psyched.

"It's a physical game, but a great receiver, you tell him you're going to drop the next pass, and he might drop the next pass.

"There are legal ways you can get cheap shots on guys. Not that I would do it. Technically, if a receiver doesn't catch a pass, he's a blocker. Intimidation makes the game fun and interesting for me."

"Do you like the safety blitz?" I asked the man who looked like the barkeep at the best watering spot on Bourbon Street.

"I love it," said Harris.

"Favorite play?"

"Yeah."

"Why?"

"It gets me close to the quarterback."

"Doesn't Craig know your act?"

"I wouldn't try to psyche Craig," said Harris, and the sarcasm dripped.

"It's not important. It's just the Super Bowl."

◆   ◆   ◆

I went back to the hotel, wrote, filed the column and called the office in Detroit. The editor told me the Lions had called a press conference for Wednesday morning. Here I was once again at the Super Bowl, out of town, and the story was breaking back home. But not all of it. The Bills had called a press conference in Buffalo, too.

This was one night I did not stay out late on Bourbon Street.

The Crushed Orange

I was awake early at the Hyatt. I hopped the bus downstairs and rode out to the Broncos' headquarters. I was hopped-up myself. The breakfast spread the NFL put on at the Broncos included eggs benedict, which was not for me. I headed for a pay phone in the lobby. The office confirmed the details for me. Monte Clark was the new coach of the Detroit Lions. Chuck Knox had been hired by the Buffalo Bills. How smug could I be!

"Stop preening, showboat," my friend New York yelped at me.

"Is the Greek in town yet?" I muttered.

I called the Lions' office in Detroit to talk to Clark. He would be my column subject today — no Cowboys, no Broncos.

"Thanks for not denying the story when I called you last time," I said to Clark.

"I tried to help you as best I could," Clark responded. "I'll be going down to New Orleans and see you there."

I floated, gloated back into the Broncos' interview room, just to listen.

The bloody Lions couldn't get to play in one, but once again they'd upstaged the Super Bowl.

◆　　◆　　◆

This time Pete Rozelle had really come up with a gimmick for his Super Bowl: the Broncos!

My mind dug back into the history of the American Football League, vanished years earlier in the merger. The Denver Broncos were the symbol of the AFL to those of us with NFL roots. They came with the AFL's charter — a team of culls and rejects, athletes who could never qualify for NFL clubs such as Detroit and Philadelphia. They were imports who had played in Canada and kids such as Gene Mingo, who wrote a letter while he was still a sailor in the U.S. Navy, begging for a tryout. The owners dressed their Broncos in gold jerseys and brown pants. Their socks had thick vertical stripes. Not even Pete Rozelle had ever seen a football team wearing socks with up-and-down stripes. The NFL establishment giggled at Denver. So did most of the AFL.

The club did not have a playbook. It could barely afford a football.

The 1960 schedule called for the Broncos to play in the first game ever contested by the AFL, on a Friday night in Boston. The Broncos showed up in their grotesque regalia, and everybody laughed. The football players looked like they'd emerged from old tintype photographs from the 1920s. The Broncos were 16-point underdogs. Mingo ran a punt back 76 yards for a touchdown. The Broncos defeated the Patriots, 13-10. The AFL had been launched.

Within a year, the club was nearly bankrupt. The team was about to be moved to San Antonio. Some local Denver money was plunged into the franchise, and the AFL kept it in the Rocky Mountains. The Broncos played through the '60s with a series of 2-11-1 and 3-10 seasons. When the NFL annexed the AFL as part of the merger, the Broncos trailed along. As full partners, the Broncos of the early '70s, now dressed in bright orange and blue, had improved their standards to five victories in a season. It was 1973 when the Broncos, at last, finished a season with their first winning record. They were 7-5-2 under John Ralston.

Ralston went on TV and promised the Denver people: "Twelve and two and on to the Super Bowl."

The Broncos skidded backward.

Three years later Ralston was dumped in a revolt by his players. Ralston had come out of Stanford to coach in the pros with a Dale Carnegie approach. The players mocked Ralston. He had spent 13 years in the off-season teaching motivational theory for the Dale Carnegie organization. But he wasn't able to teach motivation during the season.

"Everybody laughed at us," the bearded, angry Lyle Alzado told the writers. "People in restaurants would come up to us and say, `twelve and two and on to the Super Bowl,' and laugh.

"When we were on the field and looked to the sidelines for leadership, there was nobody to give it. Our coach was running up and down the sidelines cheerleading. Nobody was coaching."

I started taking notes.

"Our offense was a predictable ballet," said Billy Thompson, a veteran defensive back. "One, two, three, kick. One, two, three, kick."

A dozen anarchists met in secret after the 1976 season — Alzado, Armstrong, Thompson, Tom Jackson, Haven Moses and Gradishar among them — and drafted an anti-Ralston statement despite an improved 9-5 record. They leaked it to the press.

It said: "We don't believe it is possible to win a championship under the guidance of John Ralston. He has lost the respect of the players and we don't believe he is capable of leading us to a championship."

"That Dale Carnegie stuff was all bullshit," said Alzado at Super Bowl XII, slipping into falsetto. "'Hey man, we're gonna do better today than yesterday.'"

And Red Miller became the coach.

◆　　◆　　◆

It is not known for sure if Pete Rozelle emitted a mighty cheer when the Cowboys qualified for Super Bowl XII on New Year's Day 1978. Bud Grant put that thought in our craggy heads. Pete wanted theater in his Super Bowl, not purple patsies.

The Cowboys went click, click, click with typical precision through the NFC season with a 12-2 record. They didn't have to breathe hard. They reached the playoffs for the 11th time in 12 seasons, a remarkable feat in a bang-up sport with a draft aimed toward producing artificial parity. They had their Staubach, and he was playing with veteran's brilliance now. But the root of their success was their wisdom in the draft. Now again, with Gil Brandt's input, Loophole Schramm and Smilin' Tom Landry had come up with a coup. They had gotten Tony Dorsett, the Heisman

Trophy runner, by jumping all the way up the draft rotation. Dorsett was worked into Landry's complex scheme slowly, efficiently. He was prepared to use his slippery skills in the playoffs.

So the Cowboys polished off the Bears 37-7 in the first playoff game. They would play the Vikings in the NFC championship game.

The NFL was confronted again with — ugh — the possibility of the Vikings going back for their fifth Super Bowl. The simple mathematical fact was, for the Vikings to go 0-4 in Super Bowls, they had to go 4-0 in NFC championship games.

Bud Grant told us at Dallas before the NFC championship game: "I'm not sure the league is particularly happy that we're in the playoffs. They'd rather have the glamour teams. I don't think we have the charisma as a team that some of the other clubs do."

Nobody could tell for sure if Bud had his tongue in his cheek. But the world was spared from having to stuff down the Vikings at another Super Bowl. The Vikings had peaked a game early versus Dallas. They fumbled the ball away a couple of times and their defense went plop. The Cowboys won it 23-6 to qualify for their own fourth Super Bowl.

In Denver, there was a new insanity known as Broncomania. The townspeople displayed a permanent extended finger to the rest of Pro Football America. It was not the finger folks customarily use for such gestures, but rather the index finger. Number one. The people clad themselves in orange — orange fools' caps, orange drawers, orange T-shirts, orange nightshirts. The defense, led by Alzado and Jackson and Gradishar, was referred to as the Orange Crush.

And crush it did. The Broncos crashed through the AFC season with a 12-2 record.

"Broncomania is more than just something happening in Denver and Colorado," my old AFL friend Denver told me as we hit Bourbon Street one night. "Broncomania now covers Wyoming and Utah and Idaho."

"Shoot, man," I responded. "Broncomania right now is native America — as much as the Wild West, Manhattan Island and the Golden Gate Bridge. People can identify with the Broncos. With flesh, with the downtrodden."

In the postseason playoffs for the first time ever, the Broncos beat the muscle of Pittsburgh, 34-21. Then they played the Raiders for the AFC championship. In the third quarter, Rob Lytle, Denver's top runner, coughed the ball up. It was an obvious fumble. Mike McCoy recovered it for the Raiders as John Madden floated for joy on the sideline and Al Davis clenched a happy fist in the press box. But on the field, Ed

> *"Everybody said it would be a cold day in hell if the Broncos got into the playoffs...Everybody said it would be a cold day in hell if we got to the Super Bowl. Well, we made the devil wear an overcoat."*
> — *Denver veteran Billy Thompson*

Marion, the head linesman, waved off the fumble recovery. He had blown his whistle before the ball popped loose. The play was dead; Denver retained possession. The TV replays clearly showed a fumble, but there was no rule allowing a reversal. The Broncos went on to score a touchdown; they went on to win the AFC championship game, 20-17; they went on to Super Bowl XII. Denver went crazy. So did Al Davis. People said there ought to be some way to review disputed calls by reviewing TV replays. Others said that would be folly and would never be included in Pete Rozelle's rules.

Billy Thompson had played through the terrible years with the Broncos. He was a nine-year veteran, and now he was at the Super Bowl surrounded by writers from across America.

"Everybody said it would be a cold day in hell if the Broncos got into the playoffs," Thompson told us. "Everybody said it would be a cold day in hell if we won a game in the playoffs. Everybody said it would be a cold day in hell if we got to the Super Bowl."

Thompson grinned at the whole bunch of us.

"Well, we made the devil wear an overcoat."

The Broncos possessed some sort of dirty-faced appeal. What was it? They made you laugh. They tugged at your sympathy strings. They were life's clobbered souls risen for their hurrah, at last.

If only all those orange-clad bumpkins didn't tag along.

The Broncos came to the Super Bowl banking on a reformed mugger and barroom bouncer, a mortician, a refugee from the Pottstown Firebirds and World Football League, and a born-again quarterback.

Lyle Alzado was the onetime mugger and bouncer. He now led locker room coups.

The mortician was named Godwin Turk. He said: "I like funeral homes and always have. I just started as a kid. I learned from the bottom up. I started washing hearses, making runs and picking bodies up. I was in the 10th grade before I started putting my hands on them." Turk planned to use his Super Bowl earnings as a partial payment on a funeral home in Houston.

Jack Doblin, a receiver, had gone from the Pottstown Firebirds of the sandlot leagues to the Chicago Fire of the short-lived World Football League to the Broncos to the Super Bowl. That was better than his real-life job of cracking bones as a chiropractor.

And the born-again quarterback was Craig Morton, now 35, who had been chased at Dallas years before by Staubach. Morton had been excellent in the season and the playoffs, beating Oakland with a very sore hip that further limited his limited mobility. Poor Craig, he was as the Super Bowl with the IRS safety blitzing him for payment of back taxes.

He was told that Cliff Harris, his supposed friend, had put a bounty out on him for the Super Bowl. Morton replied: "That's a stupid thing to say."

◆   ◆   ◆

It was broad daylight as I pushed my way down Bourbon Street. The crowds were thick, and everyone carried the now traditional plastic cups in their hands. Football had become America's excuse to get drunk. And it seemed as if all of Denver was clogged into this street — the yahoos in their orange cowboy hats, their orange sweatshirts, their orange pants, their orange skins. Monte Clark was at the Royal Sonesta, ready to meet the emigres in the Detroit press who had skipped town early to cover the Super Bowl.

Jimmy the Greek was in the lobby. He was talking about 300 million dollars being bet on the Super Bowl. I approached him with a nickel-full of tact.

"I guess I was the one who had it right," I said. "Clark to the Detroit, Knox to Buffalo."

"Hmmmmph," responded the Greek.

Pete Rozelle's party was held on the banks of the Mississippi at the Rivergate Convention Center. The theme, as expected in New Orleans, was jazz. The food was Cajun.

Rozelle's party planners really missed it. King Tut was in town this Super Bowl week. I had gone out to the Treasures of Tutankhamen at the New Orleans Museum of Art for guidance in making my prediction for the dollar Super Bowl press pool. Looking at King Tut's mummified face amid his 3,000-year-old Egyptian playthings, I said: "How do you see it, Tut?"

I heard a deep voice respond, I think: "Don't believe the books, lad. Take the Cowboys and the points."

The Greek had made the Cowboys five-point favorites.

"Most of all, beware of Greeks bearing gifts," the deep voice seemed to tell me.

King Tut's tomb might have been the best Super Bowl party scene ever. Pete's planners blew it.

The sun appeared on Sunday after another cold, dreary Louisiana Super Bowl week. But climate did not matter. Super Bowl XII was staged indoors, in the monolithic Superdome. No blimp. No Air Force flyovers. No bus rides, either. We walked over a bridge from the Hyatt to the football game.

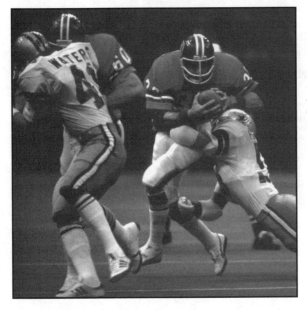

*Running back Otis
Armstrong tries to
elude Dallas
defenders.
(Photo©Vernon
Biever)*

Tom Landry started Super Bowl XII with a gimmick. A double reverse put the ball into the hands of Butch Johnson, a wide receiver. Butch dropped it and got it back as Jackson and the orange-suited Broncos dove for it. Lucky for Dallas, the play lost only 9 yards.

But again the trend of the Super Bowl had been established. Dallas punted. Denver moved to the Cowboys' 33, and Morton was tossed for an 11-yard loss. Denver punted, and Tony Hill tried to field it at his 1 rather than letting it bounce harmlessly into the end zone. Hill fumbled. Three Broncos dove for the ball. Hill recovered it. Then Dorsett, a touchdown hero in his first playoffs, fumbled. The Cowboys recovered again. Then they punted.

Now Morton had the ball. He stepped back to pass, and Harvey Martin and Randy White rushed in on him for the line. Craig threw. Randy Hughes intercepted at the 25. Staubach is death when given the opportunity. He took the Cowboys in for a touchdown, scored from the 3 by Dorsett.

Moments later Morton was intercepted a second time, by Aaron Kyle. This time Staubach got the Cowboys a field goal, a 35-yarder kicked by Efren Herrera. The Broncos were down 10-zip in the first quarter.

14

In the second quarter Herrera kicked a 43-yard field goal for a 13-0 lead.

Red Miller ordered Morton to throw the bomb to the streaking Haven Moses. Moses beat the cornerback, Bennie Barnes. Morton underthrew the ball and was intercepted a third time. Dallas had to punt. Downfield, John Schultz waited to field the football. The ball hit him in the head, on the helmet with the bucking bronco etched upon it. Dallas recovered. The Cowboys failed to score more.

Morton connected on a pass to Doblin, the escapee from the Pottstown Firebirds and WFL. Doblin fumbled the ball. Dallas recovered. The Orange Crush halted Dallas. Morton connected on a pass to Riley Odoms. Odoms fumbled the ball. Dallas recovered.

Just before halftime, Morton passed again. Mark Washington grabbed it, and Morton had been intercepted for a fourth time.

At last the clock ran down, and it was finally halftime. Denver had been lucky to be down 13-0 after seven turnovers. Herrera had missed two field goals, and the Cowboys also had fumbled the ball away at the Denver 12. Miller told Morton in the locker room he would be starting the second half, but if the Broncos failed to move, he'd be yanked.

The Broncos moved, slightly. Morton got them into field-goal range. Jim Turner, point scorer in Super Bowl III for the Jets, kicked a 47-yarder. But then Staubach, on a pass play he made up in the huddle, hit Butch Johnson 45 yards downfield. Butch dove and caught the ball at the goal line. Dallas was up 20-3.

Morton tried again. He threw. Too Tall Jones reached for the pass and missed it, nearly interception No. 5. That was it. Miller benched his quarterback — true to the words of Cliff Harris that Morton would not finish the game. Norris Weese took over and guided the Broncos to a touchdown in four more plays. Lytle scored from the 1. Denver was behind by 10 again, and the Broncos had been a fourth-quarter team. But then Weese fumbled the ball away.

Denver quarterback Craig Morton's (7, above) stability through the regular season and the playoffs helped propel the Broncos to the Super Bowl, but after four first-half interceptions, he was replaced by Norris Weese (right) who had no better luck against the Cowboys than Morton. Here Weese feels the pressure exerted by Dallas' Ed "Too Tall" Jones.(Photos©Vernon Biever)

Landry went to the halfback pass, and Robert Newhouse fired a floater that Golden Richards caught to produce a 29-yard touchdown.

That was it and Pete Rozelle's 12th Super Bowl showcase ended with two quarterbacks who came out of the WFL circus — Weese and Dallas's Danny White — rolling around, groping for bouncing footballs. The final was Dallas 27, Denver 10; and, the Cowboys had broken the AFC's string of five consecutive Super Bowl victories.

As it ended, a Dallas linebacker named Hollywood Henderson crumpled an orange cup in his fist and thrust it at the crowd and yelled: "There's your orange crush."

◆   ◆   ◆

Tom Landry had been immortalized with his second Super Bowl victory, joining the Great Lombardi, Don Shula and Chuck Noll.

Landry was plastic when asked if he was proud to be joining the legends.

"Not really," he twanged. "I don't have goals like that."

Perhaps it was a reaction to the quality of the football. Between them the Super Bowl teams managed 10 fumbles, four pass interceptions, 20 penalties and three missed field-goal attempts.

NEW ORLEANS — This was the Super Bowl, honest injun!

I know that to be a fact, because at halftime Pete Rozelle recreated the Follies Bergeres for the millions tucked away in their living rooms across America. Once before Pete had recreated the Battle of New Orleans and the cannon went off and the horse bolted tossing the cavalryman into the end zone.

One of these years Pete ought to recreate a pro football game at the Super Bowl — just to provide something different.

To the Victor

Go the Spoils

John Elway was standing in the middle of Fifty-third Street, Manhattan, New York City, USA, tossing footballs through a hoop held by fitness maven Richard Simmons, dressed in what appeared to be sequinned underwear. The footballs traveled a couple of sewers in distance, New Yorkese for manhole covers.

"A longtime tradition," David Letterman told his giggling audience. "The Late Night Quarterback Challenge."

A live mob kept on the sidewalks by barriers, night creatures across America's TV realm, watched with great eagerness.

Going to Disneyland, a hometown parade, an invitation to the Letterman show — these are all part of the booty awarded annually to the winning quarterback of the Super Bowl.

The quarterback gets to play in burlesque. They are gigs that pay, the spoils of victory. Troy Aikman did it. Steve Young did it. Bret Favre did it. Joe Montana — they all did it.

Now after his 15 seasons, John Elway received invitations that he could not turn down. It is part of the ritual. In the aftermath, there is the lampoon.

And in the aftermath, there is the serious admission. The relief expressed by John Elway that he had joined the Super Bowl winning quarterbacks. At last.

"You're never going to be up there with the elite quarterbacks without winning the Super Bowl," Elway said to the journalistic mob in the interview tent rigged on the Qualcomm Stadium parking lot following Denver's victory.

It was the first time he had spoken such words.

"My career would not have been complete without this," he said.

"I only want to say four words," Pat Bowlen, the Broncos' owner, said when Commissioner Paul Tagliabue presented the Vince Lombardi Trophy — the championship silver. "This one's for John."

Four, for sure.

The game is victories. Victories and money and there is a correlation. John Elway has won the most pro football games of any quarterback who ever cranked up his arm and threw a forward pass. More than Montana. More than Terry Bradshaw. More than Bart Starr. More than John Unitas. More than Sid Luckman. More than anybody since the pro league was founded in the Hupmobile auto agency in Canton, Ohio, back in 1920.

He entered the Super Bowl with 138 victories in his career. But one had eluded him through the 15 years, with three losses etched into his career profile. He was smothered with the stigma that he had never won a Super Bowl.

The money factor is this: Elway lowered his 1987 salary to permit Neil Smith to join the Broncos and strengthen the team's defense and fit in under the NFL's stringent salary cap. The money was ticketed to Elway in the future.

In prelude to Super Bowl XXXII, Elway spoke during his press sessions of his maturing process and past pain:

"I've learned perspective. You get married, have a family, do different things outside of football. Early in my career football was it for me, my only priority. I put all my importance on winning the Super Bowl.

"Not that it isn't a high priority with me now. But it's not the most important."

He had spoken those words to a mob that first circus day of Super Bowl XXXII about feeling the wrath of a city. He had been beaten three times at the Super Bowl, outclassed, twice by lesser quarterbacks. Phil Simms had played the game of his life when the Giants beat the Broncos, 39-20. And Doug Williams never before nor ever after played as brilliantly as he did when the Redskins beat the Broncos, 42-10. Only Joe Montana played quarterback with the quality of John Elway. And Montana had had a vintage day when the 49ers beat the Broncos in Super Bowl XXIV, 55-10.

Along with the wrath Elway felt the cloying, smothering feeling of celebrity in Denver.

I remember visiting Denver in the summer of 1983, when the weather was scorching. I went for a football game. The city was the site of the first United States Football League championship game, a spring/summer league that briefly challenged the NFL. The Michigan Panthers were playing the Philadelphia Stars. There would be national TV.

But the Denver newspapers subordinated this game — and whatever else was going on in the world — to herald the arrival of John Elway, the rookie quarterback. The Broncos were opening camp in Greeley, I think it was, and all the prominent Denver sports media were out of town for the Panthers vs. the Stars.

At this time, Elway had finagled his way to the Broncos.

He was a West Coast kid, son of a football coach, Jack Elway. His father — now the Broncos director of pro scouting — was a football coach. He would become head coach at San Jose State. Son John elected to play his college ball at Stanford.

Jack Elway, quoted in the *Rocky Mountain News*, has frequently said about himself: "Jack, old boy, you've got to be the dumbest SOB in the whole world. You have the best quarterback in America and you let him get away."

John would become an All-American at Stanford, plus a fine-hitting baseball player. George Steinbrenner drafted and signed him as an outfielder for the Yankees. He might have made it. He played some minor-league ball, batting .318 for Oneonta in the New York-Penn League before his senior football season at Stanford.

In the NFL, the Baltimore Colts had the first pick of '83 — and they selected Elway. Six quarterbacks were drafted that year, among them Jim Kelly, Tony Eason and Dan Marino. All would lose in Super Bowls.

Elway refused to sign with the Colts. Their coach was Frank Kush, who had a tyrant's profile similar to Vince Lombardi's but not a similar record.

John refused and refused — and at last the Colts put him up for trade. The maneuvering turned frantic in the NFL inner sanctums. The Raiders and the Chargers were among the supplicants. Finally, the Broncos acquired him May 2, 1983. It was a whopper of a trade. The Broncos gave up Chris Hinton, their first-round draftee of '83, their 1984 draft choice, backup quarterback Mark Herrmann plus a million bucks cash.

Elway would become a great bargain in the quarterback lore of pro football. And there is an extensive list of such quarterbacks who would become champions — free-agent John Unitas, released by the Steelers; 17th-round draft choice Bart Starr and third-round draftee Joe Montana.

Soon Elway won AFC championships and was adored by a city. His family — wife Janet, their three daughters and a son — were required to live fish-bowl lives. Elway himself would have to go to the barber's home to get his hair cut. Too many fawning fans at the barber shop.

"You kind of become numb to it," Elway said about the autographs and the grabbing and the interviews in comments in San Diego. "It's not easy to go get gas, go get doughnuts, go get coffee.

"You're not allowed to be in a bad mood. There are times when you just don't want to talk.

"Probably the hardest thing is having kids. You won't be able to go where your kids want to go. Usually, when you go to those places, there are lots of other kids, and what were toys become secondary to me.

"I become the toy."

Throughout, there was the slicing reminder: Can Elway be considered great if he never wins a Super Bowl?

In the pomp and circumstance, in the buildup to Super Bowl XXXII, Elway was being judged daily by the nation and its media on his failures rather than his successes. It was unfair, this measurement, but we are the media and sometimes we tilt in a cock-eyed fashion.

"I've never been able to live those down," Elway told the press. "I'd like to get it behind me, but it's not allowed.

"All you've got to do is win it once. A win would redeem the losses."

He has been redeemed. Proof is one appearance with David Letterman on Fifty-third Street in New York, throwing footballs in a burlesque at Richard Simmons.

A Super Bull Market

While there is no reason to believe a professional football should have a bearing on the stock market, it is hard to find a better indicator than the Super Bowl Theory. The Super Bowl Indicator holds that a victory by an NFC team or an original (pre-1970 merger) NFL team — the Browns, Colts or Steelers — would point to a bullish market for the following year. A victory by an AFC team would be a bearish signal and indicate a drop in the market by the end of the calendar year. Since 1967, the Super Bowl Theory has been accurate 28 times.

Year/SB	Dow Jones Close	Indicator	Winner
1967/I	905.11	Up	Packers, NFL
1968/II	943.75	Up	Packers, NFL
1969/III	800.36	Down	Jets, AFL
1970/IV	838.92	Up	Chiefs, AFL*
1971/V	890.20	Up	Colts, old NFL
1972/VI	1020.02	Up	Cowboys, NFC
1973/VII	850.38	Down	Dolphins, AFC
1974/VIII	815.24	Down	Dolphins, AFC
1975/IX	852.41	Up	Steelers, old NFL
1976/X	1004.65	Up	Steelers, old NFL
1977/XI	831.17	Down	Raiders, AFC
1978/XII	805.01	Down	Cowboys, NFC*
1979/XIII	838.74	Up	Steelers, old NFL
1980/XIV	963.99	Up	Steelers, old NFL
1981/XV	875.00	Down	Raiders, AFC
1982/XVI	1046.55	Up	49ers, NFC
1983/XVII	1258.64	Up	Redskins, NFC
1984/XVIII	1211.57	Down	Raiders, AFC
1985/XIX	1546.67	Up	49ers, NFC
1986/XX	1895.95	Up	Bears, NFC
1987/XXI	1938.83	Up	Giants, NFC
1988/XXII	2168.57	Up	Redskins, NFC
1989/XXIII	2753.20	Up	49ers, NFC
1990/XXIV	2633.66	Down	49ers, NFC*
1991/XXV	3168.83	Up	Giants, NFC
1992/XXVI	3301.11	Up	Redskins, NFC
1993/XXVII	3754.09	Up	Cowboys, NFC
1994/XXVIII	3834.44	Up	Cowboys, NFC
1995/XXIX	5117.12	Up	49ers, NFC
1996/XXX	6448.27	Up	Cowboys, NFC
1997/XXXI	7908.25	Up	Packers, NFC

*Indicator Incorrect

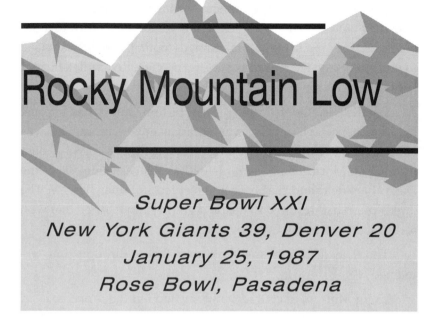

Rocky Mountain Low

Super Bowl XXI
New York Giants 39, Denver 20
January 25, 1987
Rose Bowl, Pasadena

The logistics for a southern California Super Bowl are the most difficult because of the vastness of the territory, the gridlock on the freeways, the smog, the noxious fumes. The NFL — with a piquant touch of irony — billeted the Super Bowl press down the street from Disneyland.

We were handy to a variety of interview subjects — John Elway, Phil Simms, Donald Duck. In the evening, we had our choice of Mexican restaurants.

The first thing you noticed about John Elway was his teeth. In NFL circles, there was occasional debate about the might of his arm. But there was total agreement about the dazzling qualities of John's enormous smile.

New York, chic and smart, was in this Super Bowl, versus Denver, which was nestled into the Rocky Mountains, a lost city of yahoos dressed in bright orange with deep emotions for a collection of football mercenaries. There was nothing blase about Denver. Nine years earlier, Denver had brought its ever-loving hordes of pumpkin-tinted bumpkins to a Super Bowl and had gone away embarrassed.

Through the years, the Broncos managed to remain competi-tive; they were a challenging team that yearned to return to a Su-per Bowl. They made the annual changes football teams must make to prevent decay. There was a coaching change. Red Miller, the old fist-faced fighter, was gone.

Dan Reeves, sophisticated protege of Tom Landry, had become the Broncos' head coach. He was experienced in winning. He was experienced in Super Bowls. Once upon a time, a forward pass from Craig Morton had been misfired as Reeves came out of the Dallas backfield and had been intercepted in Super Bowl V. The interception had resulted in the field goal by Jim O'Brien that won for the Colts, over the Cowboys.

The thread, connecting the Super Bowls through time, re-mained.

Craig Morton, of course, had long ago left the Broncos.

The basic reason the Broncos kept their edge through the sea-sons was John Elway. He had been drafted tops off the board out of Stanford by the Baltimore Colts in 1983. It was the year Dan Marino almost got lost. John, educated, California-raised, did not quite recognize the appeal of Chesapeake Bay crabcakes. He flatly refused to play pro football in Baltimore. The town would soon be abandoned anyway when the entire load of property owned by the Colts would be dumped aboard moving vans in the middle of the night and taken to Indianapolis. The Colts had been forced to trade Elway's rights to Denver. His toothy caricature promptly became as significant to pro football as the NFL's badge-shaped logo.

Elway was a pro football star the first day he dressed in Denver's pumpkin orange with the number 7 on his chest. Maga-zine, television and newspaper media from as far away as America's command center in New York gravitated to the Bron-cos' Rocky Mountains hideaway. Just to schmooze with Elway.

Elway started as a rookie. His arm threw passes with the ve-locity of a fired cannon shell. But without the accuracy. Not to worry, there was no NFL quarterback with more potential. John played with derring-do. He scooted out of the pocket. He ran the ball, daring linebackers to belt him. He slid across the turf. His passes singed the fingers of his receivers. And as the seasons passed, John developed a tendency for the absurdly dramatic on the football field. The Broncos were in Super Bowl XXI simply because Elway had managed to succeed on a 98-yard march in frigid conditions in an enemy town against the clock — to survive in the AFC championship game.

> *"You can't believe the pressure John has been under ever since he joined our team."*
> — *Dan Reeves, Denver head coach*

"You can't believe the pressure John has been under ever since he joined our team," said Reeves.

Now Elway, his teeth, his arm, his personality, his characteristics, were under the magnifying glass of a Super Bowl. New York, where all the publicity drums were in business, was in it. But the show in this Super Bowl prelude would be a kid who played in Denver. Somewhere across the Hudson River — America's continental divide — out there in the mountains.

◆   ◆   ◆

The Super Bowl 2,000 milled around on the parking lot at Cal State-Irvine. It was another Super Bowl picture day. The sun beat on us as we were kept captive on the bubbling asphalt of the parking lot. My mind retreated to another picture day, five years earlier, when we had been corralled to wait for the players to be uncaged for our grilling. We'd nearly suffered frostbite that Super Bowl day in Pontiac. Now we risked sunstroke as we awaited the Giants.

The Giants were this season's Chicago Bears, remodeled. They played football with that much gristle. Their game was bloody noses and sticks in the gut. And they had peaked when it was best to peak. The Giants were on a roll — rolling toward the Super Bowl. This mighty roll made them true successors to the Bears of the year before. There was no doubt in my mind that the Giants would be able to tease, to toy, to frolic with the Broncos, just as the Bears had with the Patriots.

But as another Super Bowl week started, the Giants were there, and they hadn't been immortalized on videotape. They went to the Super Bowl — but without a Refrigerator. Their defensive celebrity did have a nickname. Lawrence Taylor was called by his initials.

Their quarterback did not sport headbands and punker's eyeshades and show up in stretch jumpsuits with advertisements on his chest. He did not transport his acupuncturist to California. Phil Simms came out of Kentucky, and he was full of "Aw, shucks."

"We didn't make the Super Bowl Shuffle," said Bart Oates, the Giants' center. "We may be boring — boring from a Fifth Avenue standpoint. We don't have anybody endorsing clothes. But what we have here fits perfectly."

There was no trickery to the plays when Joe Morris was handed the football. He was as subtle as the guy lugging a lunch bucket into a factory on the morning shift.

"This team is very blue-collar," Morris said. "That's because Bill Parcells is a blue-collar coach.

"When I started out here with this team, we were 4-5. Then we were 3-12-1. For somebody who's been here through the lean times, this means a lot. They said we'd never do it."

It was a grinder's team. Joe Morris did not wear Calvin Kleins in Calvin Klein's own town. Joe wore Levis.

The Giants had been put down, knocked down, for a generation. All they heard through the years of travail was the glorious history of the old Giants.

They heard the comic stories. How one Sunday, the Giants were endeavoring to run out the last minute to preserve a victory over the Eagles. How Joe Pisarcik, the quarterback, fumbled a handoff. How the Eagles grabbed the fumble and ran it back for a touchdown, the touchdown that beat the Giants.

How an airplane flew over Giants Stadium trailing a banner: "Fifteen years of losing football — we've had enough."

How the fans booed Phil Simms the day he was drafted from college.

◆　　◆　　◆

The Giants hadn't been champions since 1956, when Frank Gifford lugged the ball. It was a decade before the creation of the Super Bowl, back in the Dark Ages, as Joe Morris called that time in history. The days of Gifford and Charley Conerly and Y.A. Tittle, and before them Tuffy Leemans and Ken Strong and Ward Cuff.

The Giants, just as the Bears, came to the Super Bowl with a rich tradition, followed by years of poverty. "All they used to talk about was the old days," Morris said. "Now people are going to talk about this team."

Among those talking would be Gifford, who wore a fur coat to the New Jersey Meadowlands the day the Giants qualified for the Super Bowl.

The Giants permitted themselves only one escape from normalcy. When they won, which was practically every Sunday, they committed the juvenile delinquent's act of drenching their coach with Gatorade. Bill Parcells always laughed as he dodged Harry Carson's splashing bucket.

Somehow, the TV cameras always had Carson and Parcells in focus when the bucket was turned over. Somehow.

Alert media are the salvation of a bug-eyed nation.

◆　　◆　　◆

The NFL put John Elway and the Broncos up in Newport Beach. This slice of swank had grown in snootiness since Super Bowl V and the press stayed there. We came, as always, by bus. And every morning Elway would arrive, flashing the grin in his boy's face. And 200 TV cameras would trail him, their operators banging each other for position. For the welfare of the bug-eyed nation.

Elway would pop out the platitudes. "I've always wondered," spoke John to the vast assemblage, "does anyone ever reach his potential?"

It would have been a disservice to the clientele not to write about Elway.

NEWPORT BEACH, Calif. — QB VII went to Hollywood by limousine to meet Eddie Murphy filming Beverly Hills Cop II *during hype time of Super Bowl XXI.*

"I got up there and said 'I'm sure glad I'm a football player and not an actor,'" said John Elway, QB, with No. 7 on his football shirt. "It takes forever to set up one shot."

Elway, it is recalled, can move 98 yards lugging a football and an entire team in barely a minute and some fractions. He speaks cleaner than Eddie Murphy, too.

"I like to go out and have a beer with the guys," said Elway, getting about as raunchy as he can get.

Super Bowl XXI is about to drop on us with its glitzy thud. John Elway is the star. He's the attraction. They've put his name on the marquee at the Rose Bowl: "JOHN ELWAY VS. THE GIANTS, Sunday, 3 p.m."

What the Giants will do to John Elway is something else. But this is the Super Bowl. He appears with a cast of . . . well, 44 (XLIV). It is John Elway and the spear carriers. Those extras who are role players for the Broncos.

The guys, as John Elway calls them.

This is a rare football team, the Broncos. There is no resentment. It lacks jealousy. The Giants may be brutes, tough guys who want to kick in Elway's mouthful of teeth. The Broncos are class.

"John's won a few ballgames for us," said Steve Watson, who gets so little publicity for making his acrobatic pass catches. "We're excited for John. We never look at it with jealousy. We know his attitude. He wants to be one of us."

The Broncos went to the Super Bowl once before. It was nine years ago . . . Denver reached that Super Bowl by virtue of its defense. Orange Crush, it was called. After that Super Bowl, the Denver team was divided. The Denver defense hated the Denver offense. The guys didn't go drink beer together.

Now the Orange Crush defense adores John Elway . . .

The day John Elway marched the Broncos 98 yards against vanishing time all the way to Super Bowl XXI he did it without the limo. He did it in hostile conditions in Cleveland.

*"We kept getting hit with dog bones," said Watson, refer-
ring to the Clevelanders who brought along Ken-L-Ration to spur
on the Browns' Dawg Defense. "One end zone was littered with
dog bones. It's a shame I didn't have my dogs there."*

Elway was there, though. And he reached the end zone.

"No wonder we all love him," said Watson.

New York, New York, it's a wonderful town — sort of.

But there were those in New York who would never forgive
the Giants from abandoning the city and moving across the Hudson
River divide to New Jersey.

"Foreigners," Ed Koch had proclaimed before the Giants
reached the Super Bowl. Koch was the lord mayor of the city and
spokesman for all that ailed the world.

But somehow Lawrence Taylor convinced Koch that a lot of
New Yorkers still rooted for those foreigners. "And a whole lot of
them vote," L.T. said. It was then that Koch decided that the New
York Giants were — hurrah for them — New York's team. They'd
kept the city's name, after all.

"Mr. Koch, or whatever he calls himself . . . he's a great band-
stand player," said L.T.

Thus, one NYC government crisis was solved, with even a
promise of a parade for the Giants from Wall Street to City Hall,
New York.

But another crisis threatened as the Super Bowl neared. A Bowl
Warning was issued to the citizens of New York by the commis-
sioner of the city's Department of Environmental Protection.
"Think before you flush," Harvey Schultz declared as he decreed
that the day of Super Bowl XXI would be SUPER FLUSH SUN-
DAY.

"We could experience a temporary drop in water pressure in
some areas of the city if the game should be a close one," the commissioner warned. "A surge in water could occur at the final gun."

Thus, Schultz managed to get his name in the papers with the
rest of the Super Bowl hype.

◆   ◆   ◆

At the Giants' hotel in Costa Mesa, Lawrence Taylor tried to avoid the hype. He chose silence, as Duane Thomas had, as John Riggins had. He preferred to hide and study game film highlights.

One New York reporter managed to get L.T. to utter a few words about quarterbacks, such as John Elway: "I can be an S.O.B. Nasty, lousy, mean people are the guys who get the farthest. I love the contact. It makes the game real enjoyable. I can go two or three games without a kill shot. That's when the snot comes from his nose and he starts quivering on the ground. You want to run that film again and again."

Bill Parcells had some choice words, too: "The press are all communists."

We started to yearn for Jim McMahon and Joe Theismann. Instead, we had to settle for Phil Simms.

COSTA MESA, Calif. — This is Broadway Joe's game. The Super Bowl is Joe Namath stepping out of a Fort Lauderdale bar and guaranteeing victory. It is Mr. Laff's saloon and Joe and his ladies and his llama coat.

Phil Simms plays in the same town Joe Namath did. It was Joe Namath who established the Super Bowl as a fixture of Americana. The town is New York. They loved Joe there.

And Phil Simms? The first time anybody in New York ever heard of Phil Simms they booed him. It was NFL draft day, 1979. The NFL does it live in New York. The league rigs up bleachers and sets up a time clock and invites in the public. Pete Rozelle reads the names.

FIRST ROUND: "The New York Giants select Phil Simms, quarterback from Morehead State."

Two thousand New York voices erupted as one. Boooooo. It might have sounded like WHOOOOOO? But it was boo.

Welcomed, Phil Simms proceeded to play as a rookie for a flop team. He did OK, but the team gasped.

"A lot of times my rookie year, I had flashes of greatness," Simms said. "I said this game isn't as tough as it looks, next year I ought to be a hell of a player.

"Then things kind of went backwards."

The boos never stopped for Phil Simms. They didn't until this season.

. . . He is a Kentucky kid with strawberry blond hair and an innocent look. He could live next door and play for the high school down the street.

The Super Bowl is a quarterback's game. It was Joe Namath's game. It belonged to Starr and Stabler and Bradshaw and Montana and Plunkett and Theismann and Griese and Staubach and Unitas and McMahon.

Now it is John Elway's game.

Elway is the glitter at Super Bowl XXI. He brought the Broncos here on his historic, heroic 98-yard drive.

The Giants brought Phil Simms to the Super Bowl. He came along, like the baggage with the shoulder pads. But the game has to be played with somebody taking snaps and handing off and throwing the ball sometimes. So it's Simms, the plugger quarterback.

"I'm not pretty or exciting," said Phil Simms. "I'm not flash like John Elway. I'm just a lunch bucket kind of guy.

"Elway — he's an executive quarterback."

. . . The bad times went on for years after Phil Simms arrived with his ceremonious welcome. The Giants were able to string together a bunch of three and four-victory seasons. The fans got to pelting Simms with golf balls, eggs and rotten oranges. Unlike Phil's, the fans' throws were never intercepted.

Simms suffered injuries. He was benched . . .

"I thought, `Hey, this was never meant to be,'" he said.

He considered quitting.

Now he's the other quarterback at the Super Bowl. No victory guarantees for Phil Simms. Just a day's work under a blue collar, plugger's style. The Super Bowl is destined to become Phil Simms' game, too.

Tom Jackson was haunted by the memories of Super Bowl XII. It had been a galling loss to the Cowboys nine years before. Jackson was the senior member of the Broncos. The constant requirement for changes, for new talent, in the banging sport of pro

31

football had caused a massive turnover among the Broncos. Only three starters remained from Red Miller's first Denver Super Bowl team.

Now before Super Bowl XXI, America was laughing at the Broncos. Jimmy the Greek had made the Giants the favorites by 8½ points. Or, in the Denver psyche, he had made the Broncos 8½-point underdogs.

The smart guys in the press figured America had been set up for another Super Bowl comedy. The past three years, television sets had been clicked off long before there was any danger of a simultaneous national toilet flush at the final gun. And now we figured Super Bowl XXI would be little more than the Raiders over the Redskins, the 49ers over the Dolphins, the Bears over the Patriots. Routs.

Ticked off by our fears, our jokes, our predictions, Tom Jackson spoke for his team: "The hype and the glamour are what created the game. Guys who are never talked to have 100 people asking them questions this week. That creates a different intensity."

There was no balance of power in the NFL. Power rode a teeter-totter. After Vince Lombardi, the AFL/AFC had won 11 of the next 13 Super Bowls. But now, before Super Bowl XXI, it had tipped the other way. The NFC had beaten the AFC in four of the past five.

All of which made the Broncos appear as choice victims.

They resented these thoughts, because they had remained contenders, which few franchises had managed during rebuilding years. In 1986, the Broncos went 11-5 in winning the AFC West. They won with a wildly productive offense. But toward the end of the regular season, the Broncos went into a fade. They lost three of their last five games, including a 19-16 loss to the Giants.

In the playoffs, Elway took them to a 22-17 victory over New England at Mile High Stadium in Denver. That put them into the AFC championship game. But they would have to play in Cleveland — with the wind whipping off Lake Erie, on the lumpy field, before the vulgar, emotional fans. The Browns had the better record,

12-4, and had Bernie Kosar at quarterback. After 20 years of frustration, the Browns were aimed toward the Super Bowl.

The Cleveland fans barked and howled when their club went up on Kosar's 48-yard touchdown pass with less than six minutes to play. The score was 20-13, Cleveland. And they barked louder when the Broncos screwed up the kickoff and finally recovered it on the 2.

Elway conducted his huddle in his own end zone. The clock read 5:34 left. The drive began with an inauspicious pass. Elway hit back Sammy Winder for 5 yards. Along the way, Elway, trapped going back to pass, escaped for an 11-yard gain. Moments later he hit Steve Sewell for 22 yards and Watson for 12. The Broncos had reached Cleveland's 40 at the two-minute warning. Now Elway was flipped for an 8-yard loss. It was third-and-18 with 1:47 on the clock. Elway went for the entire glob on one play. He hit rookie Mark Jackson for 20 yards. At the 28 now, 1:19 left, he hit Sewell again for 14 yards and then chugged 9 more yards himself. The Broncos were at the 5 with 42 seconds left. With dog bones bouncing all around, Elway passed once more and Mark Jackson, sliding on the end zone dirt, caught the pass to tie the score. Elway had driven the Broncos the 98 yards in 15 plays.

In the overtime, he drove them again, from their 25 to the Cleveland 15. There Rich Karlis kicked the sudden-death field goal, a 33-yarder, to put the Broncos in Super Bowl XXI, by a 23-20 count.

The Giants needed no heroics to reach their first Super Bowl. Playing with blue-collar might all season, they finished their schedule with a nine-game winning streak. They were 14-2 for the season. Simms had emerged as a productive passer; Joe Morris, after a contract holdout until four hours before the opening game, had gained more than 1,500 yards. The linebacking trio of Taylor, Carl Banks and Harry Carson had slaughtered the enemy with their brutish tackling and blitzing. The Giants were at a peak when they entered the playoffs.

In their first playoff game, they destroyed the 49ers of Bill Walsh, 49-3. Simms threw four touchdown passes; Morris ran for two touchdowns; Taylor ran a pass interception back for a touchdown.

The Redskins were the Giants' opponents for the NFC championship game in the Meadowlands. It was a raw day in New Jersey, with the wind whipping confetti into the faces of the athletes. Parcells elected to kick off when the Giants won the toss. The Redskins could do nothing with the ball. The Giants were quickly ahead, led 17-0 at the half, and that was the final score. They were champions — for the first time since the Giffer played in their backfield.

◆　　　◆　　　◆

Pete Rozelle tossed one of his best parties in years. It was a victory party, sort of. The courts had destroyed the USFL. Given a plan by Donald Trump, the new league schemed to switch its games from spring and summer to fall. Trump, who had the New Jersey Generals among his properties, planned to go eye-to-eye, throat-to-throat, buck-to-buck against the NFL. The USFL sued for millions claiming that the NFL was in violation of antitrust, a monopoly.

Sure enough, the NFL was a monopoly, or so the jurors decided. Then they awarded the USFL one USA dollar, trebled for damages, for winning the court case. The USFL was left without the legendary pot.

Pete's party was at the Universal Studios in Hollywood. A tourist attraction, it was equipped for mobs. We were transported in trams through the sets, treated to the make-believe of Hollywood, taken back into history and back to the future.

Rozelle had just one wish, that only a Hollywood script could provide for: icy cold in the East, forcing folks to remain inside their homes; dusk gathering in the West; a football team driving in at the last moments of a tight game; the TV camera flashing on a place-kicker flexing his leg; a time-out and the kicker rushing onto the field. America pausing to catch its breath.

"What I want is a close game," said the Lord High Commissioner. "With cold weather in the East, we'd have a chance for record TV ratings." It was an annual wish. And he hadn't had a true, close Super Bowl game for five years.

◆　　　◆　　　◆

On Saturday afternoon, I drove out of Anaheim toward the Pacific as the sun set, a burning disk on the ocean, to the traditional party tossed by Dick and Trish Schaap. I had stopped in Beverly Hills on the way to people-watch along Rodeo Drive. The sidewalks of this fantasyland were full of people in burnt-orange T-shirts. They all had funny fantasies about the Broncos beating the Giants.

The Schapps' party was far up along the ocean in Malibu. I dropped down a dirt road to an isolated beach. Dick Schaap introduced me to one of the Giants' fans, Billy Crystal. He was serious about the game. Then, over a tub full of ice and beer, I ran into Jim O'Brien, a genuine hero of Super Bowls past. We relived — several times — the drama of the final moments of Super Bowl V. O'Brien's kick. It was a moment Pete Rozelle should have put into a time capsule.

◆　　　◆　　　◆

The buscapade left early from Anaheim, on the serendipitous freeway route plotted by Pete Rozelle's planners. We did get to the Rose Bowl. It was a glorious California day. Neil Diamond sang a glorious version of *The Star-Spangled Banner.*

The folks dressed in burnt orange were the first to show ecstasy. Elway guided the Broncos to a score on their first possession. Rich Karlis barefooted a 48-yard field goal for a 3-0 lead. Karlis was hot, first winning the game in Cleveland in sudden-death and now making this accurate kick that tied the Super Bowl record for field-goal distance.

Now Phil Simms, the jeered, ridiculed, blond quarterback, trundled onto the field and marched the Giants 78 yards. They

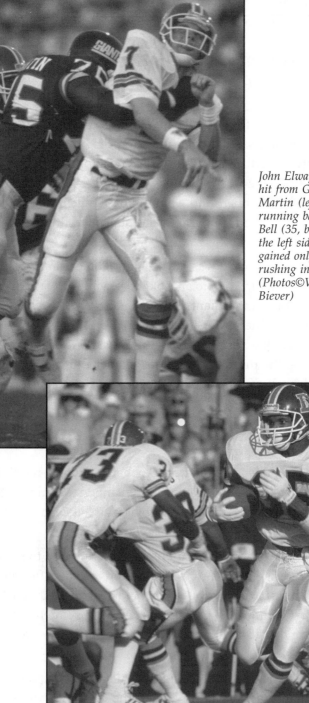

John Elway takes a hit from George Martin (left), while running back Ken Bell (35, below) tries the left side. Denver gained only 52 yards rushing in the game. (Photos©Vernon Biever)

scored the touchdown on Simms' pass to Zeke Mowatt for a 7-3 lead. Elway responded immediately, marching the Broncos 58 yards. Improvising near the goal line, Elway scored the touchdown himself on a 4-yard draw. Denver was back in front, 10-7, and form was being tossed into the ashcan.

The Broncos threatened again as the second quarter started. Elway, scooting to escape the Giants' rush, passed deep to Vance Johnson for 58 yards. Denver moved forward to a first down on the Giants' 1. Their fans were going bananas, if not oranges. Elway kept the ball on the first play, rolling right, shooting for the end zone. He met Mr. Lawrence Taylor and was flipped back for a yard loss. On second down, the Broncos tried a trap with Gerald Willhite carrying. Mr. Harry Carson stopped him for zero gain. It was third down at the 2. The Broncos tried the left side, wide this time, with Elway pitching to Sammy Winder. Mr. Carl Banks hit Winder behind the line and dragged him to the grass for a 4-yard loss.

The introductions were completed. The Broncos had met the Giants' three linebackers. The dependable Karlis went back to try the chip-shot field goal so the Broncos would not forfeit this drive without any points. Karlis missed — from the 23.

The look of the game changed. The Giants kept misfiring on offense, despite Simms' accurate passing. But the Giants' defense was nailing Elway. George Martin, the DE, loped in and trapped Elway in the end zone for a safety. The Broncos' lead was cut to 10-9. As the half ended, Karlis tried another short field goal and missed from the 34. The Broncos would have only a one-point advantage entering the second half.

Protecting that appeared impossible.

Early in the third quarter, the Broncos stopped the Giants on the far side of midfield. It was fourth down, a half-yard to go. The punting unit went onto the field. But Parcells had a trick. Backup quarterback Jeff Rutledge, on the field to block, took the snap and gained the first down. Simms capitalized immediately. He passed 12 yards to Morris, 23 to Lee Rouson, then 13 to tight end Mark Bavaro for the touchdown. Bavaro went to his knees and genuflected in the end zone. The Giants were in front, 16-10.

Mark Bavaro hoists New York Giants teammate Phil McConkey high aloft in celebration of victory in Super Bowl XXI. (Photo©Vernon Biever)

Simms would not miss. The cheers were for him. It might have sounded like music. He kept his offense going. With the lead, he marched the Giants to another score on Raul Alegre's 21-yard field goal. The Giants were ahead, 19-10. The defense was now attacking Elway, halting him. Simms got the ball again. Flipping to Morris, getting the ball returned on the flea-flicker, Simms passed deep on the old Super Bowl play that had failed once for Earl Morrall. Simms made it go, 44 yards to Phil McConkey. Morris busted over from the 1 on the next play. With 17 points in the third period, the Giants were up 26-10 entering the last quarter. Simms had passed eight-for-eight in the outburst.

And Elway couldn't hit.

Early in the fourth quarter, Simms hit the target again — Stacy Robinson for 36 yards, then McConkey for 6 on a pass that ricocheted off Bavaro for the TD. The Giants led, 33-10.

Karlis finally clicked with a 28-yarder to make a dent, nothing more. Giants, 33-13. Simms guided the Giants the distance again, Ottis Anderson scoring on a 2-yard run. Giants, 39-13.

Harry Carson edged toward the Gatorade bucket to perform the ceremonies on Parcells. Only then could Elway strike back. He hit Vance Johnson for a 47-yard touchdown before the two-minute warning. Carson edged closer, grabbed the bucket and poured over his coach. The final was 39-20, Giants, another flop for Rozelle.

But it was a piece of fine sculpture for Simms. The once-sneered-at quarterback had hit on 22 of his 25 passes in the Super Bowl. He had thrown for three touchdowns, 268 yards.

"That might be the best game a quarterback has ever played," said Parcells.

And the quarterback who had been the target of rotten fruit on his home field? He said: "When you think of the Denver Broncos, you think of John Elway. When you think of the Giants, you don't think of Phil Simms."

It still burned him. But he had burned out a segment of Giants' history for himself in the town that once cheered Tuffy Leemans, Frank Gifford and Joe Namath. Phil Simms did not leave his Super Bowl as Namath had, with the cops, the dogs, the ladies. He left in a bus. But the unlikely happened — the New York fans were pelting him with kisses and cheers.

No Time
for Mickey Mouse

Look at the coaches who have won Super Bowls.

Vince Lombardi had a gap-toothed grimace and was regarded as a fearsome tyrant. Lombardi seemed to revel in the description. "Coach treats us all the same," Henry Jordan, the Green Bay defensive tackle of Super Bowl fame, said. "Like dogs."

Chuck Noll had the physique of an offensive guard, which he was, and displayed a total lack of humor at four Super Bowls. He showed disinterest and boredom at the daily press grillings when the Steelers were in them. But Noll won all four.

Tom Landry was described as a plastic man by one of his Dallas Cowboys, Duane Thomas. And it might be the best description ever of the coach. But he won twice in the Super Bowl and might have won more.

Bill Walsh was called a genius and never disputed the notion. He won three Super Bowls with the 49ers, perhaps valid proof.

Don Shula, winner of two Super Bowls, is remembered best as the perfectionist who created the Dolphins for their perfect season.

Jimmy Johnson won two Super Bowls with the Cowboys, and his hairdo got most of the ink.

Bill Parcells also won two with the Giants and made us recoil with his sarcasm.

They were all different men, these coaches, these champion coaches of the ultimate game.

Ooops, I forgot Tom Flores, who won two Super Bowls with the Raiders — and perhaps it was because he made so little impression that he slipped from memory. After all, John Madden won one Super Bowl with the Raiders and we cannot escape him. And Al Davis owns the club.

Which brings us to Mike Shanahan.

Al Davis gave Mike Shanahan his first head coaching job in pro football, with the Raiders. In retrospect, that proves Davis' savvy in his choice of football coaching talent.

But alas, Al Davis hit a slump. He fired Shanahan after one season and four games. Davis' slump continues.

Shanahan has shown Davis that he had it right the first time.

Lombardi, Shula, Noll, Johnson, Parcells, Walsh — Shanahan is none of the above. They were pretty much the stars of their teams — with apologies to Terry Bradshaw, Bart Starr, Joe Montana, Troy Aikman and Bob Griese.

But with the Broncos, the head coach can never quite be the star, or even a co-star.

Yet before and after Super Bowl XXXII, John Elway continuously, without prompting, gave credit for the creation of a championship team to — Mike.

As an outsider, exposed to Shanahan for the first time, I found him to be matter-of-fact, devoid of color, ultra-intense, an X's and O's sort who did not relish the attention and media skirmishing of a Super Bowl.

Well, Lombardi didn't revel in it, either, and Noll purely detested it — and Marv Levy deliberately skipped Buffalo's first media day, and was fined by the NFL.

Shanahan showed up. He was assigned to Podium No. 2, which signified his rank in the pecking order as picked by the NFL publicity machine.

The coach's quotes — well, they were not scintillating, they were not controversial. He was not what we the media call GOOD PRESS.

It has taken me years, perhaps XXXII years, to realize GOOD PRESS means nothing to the fans, to the athletes, to the assistant coaches, to anybody. Except the journalists.

GOOD COACH means a hell of a lot. And that's what Mike Shanahan is.

There is, of course, the ritual that the Super Bowl victors are offered the spoils. Basking in the spotlight of victory before he ever left the field at Qualcomm Stadium, Elway said into a video cam that suddenly appeared: "I'm going to Disney Land." There is a fee for reciting those five words.

In the days before Super Bowl XXXII, Shanahan was offered a reported $30,000 to mutter the words about Disney Land or Disney World.

He stood up against blatant commercialism.

"I don't care how much they pay me," Shanahan told the journalists during a the Super Bowl prelude. "I'm not saying, 'I'm going to Disney World.'"

After all, Donald Duck cannot pass. He runs with a waddle.

Shanahan is truly the builder of Denver's champions — in the manner of Lombardi in another era in Green Bay and Shula in Miami.

As an assistant coach with the Broncos under Dan Reeves, he was part of three losses in the Super Bowl. But he trained, and perhaps tamed, Elway. Reprieved in 1995 — given a second chance to become a head coach after the fiasco period with the Raiders — he rebuilt the Broncos out of ashes. They were a 7-and-9 team on the skids when he was brought in after a spell as the 49ers' offensive wizard under George Seifert.

One of Shanahan's first acts was to draft an unsung running back named Terrell Davis. Davis was selected as the Broncos' second pick on the sixth round in 1995 — after 195 players had been taken before him.

Shanahan's second season as head coach, he guided the Broncos to their 13-3 record. His third season, 12-4 in the regular season, he won the Super Bowl.

Now Elway drew the media crowd after the victory in San Diego over the Packers. Across the press interview tent, Shanahan spoke to a smaller group. He was not the story. He did not want to be the story.

"That's been talked about since I've been in the league," Shanahan said of Denver's four lickings in earlier Super Bowls. "Any time you lose a Super Bowl you have that stigma with you. You don't have to talk about it because people talk about it constantly.

"To lose the game and not perform well is disheartening. For us to come back today and beat a team like Green Bay is very special for the team and organization."

I'll have vanilla.

The praise went to the players, in the manner of most GOOD COACHES. Elway in particular.

John Elway may have been known as a passer, but in Super Bowl XXXII, the Denver quarterback became a scrambler. He twiced rushed for first crucial first downs as well as one touchdown as he kept the Packers' defenders guessing all day. (Photo©Vernon Biever)

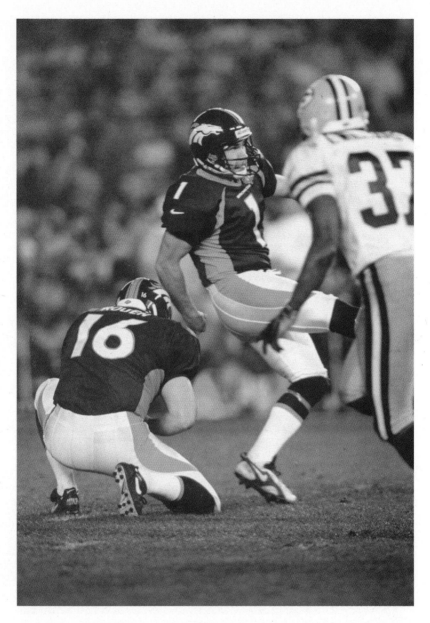

Green Bay's Tyrone Williams (37) can't get there in time as Denver kicker Jason Elam follows through on a 51-yard field goal in the second quarter of Super Bowl XXXII. It was the second-longest field goal in Super Bowl history. The holder is Tom Rouen (16). (Photo©Vernon Biever)

John Elway looks downfield for a receiver in Super Bowl XXXII. When he couldn't find a teammate to pass to, the Denver quarterback kept the Broncos in the game with his running. (Photo©James V. Biever)

Denver quarterback John Elway (7) hands off to running back Terrell Davis (30) above, while Green Bay quarterback Brett Favre looks for a receiver as Denver defender Steve Atwater (27) comes rushing in. (Both photos©James V. Biever)

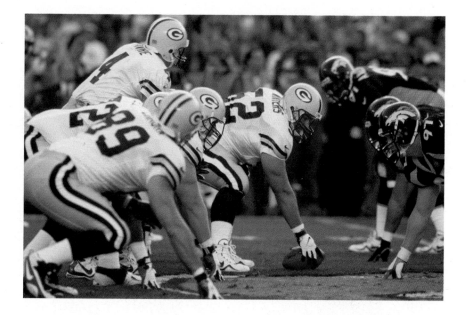

Above, Green Bay quarterback Brett Favre comes to the line under center Frank Winters as the Denver defense lines up on the other side. Below, the defense does its job as Broncos lineback John Mobley (51) wraps up Packers running back Dorsey Levens (25). (Top photo©Vernon Biever; bottom photo©James V. Biever)

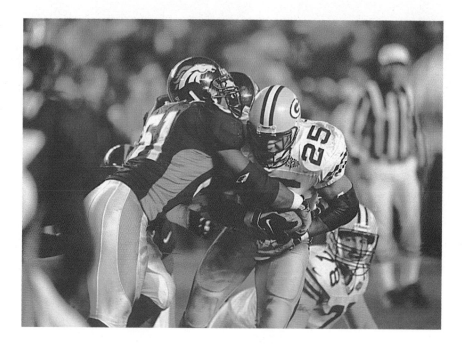

As John Elway and broadcaster Greg Gumbel look on, Denver Broncos owner Pat Bowlen holds the Super Bowl trophy while addressing the crowd after the game. (Photo©James V. Biever)

Green Bay's Doug Evans tries to corral Denver running back Terrell Davis, above. Davis sat out most of the second quarter with a migraine, but it was the Packers who ended up with a headache after Davis rushed for 157 yards on 30 carries, scored three touchdowns and was named the game's most valuable player. Below, Denver defenders Keith Traylor (94) and John Mobley (51) collapse on Green Bay running back Dorsey Levens. (Top photo©James V. Biever; bottom photo©Vernon Biever)

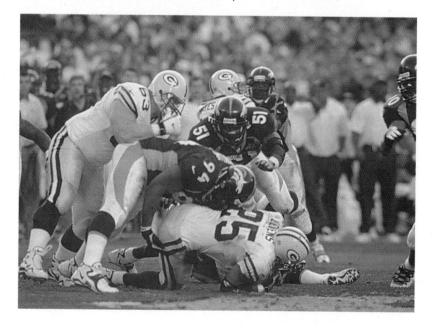

Always feared for his passing, John Elway completed 12 of 22 passes and had one interception in Super Bowl XXXII. (Photo©James V. Biever)

"The way John Elway plays exemplifies what he is," Shanahan said. "He's a competitor. He's going to throw his body on the line every time he plays. I've watched him do that since the start of his career, so today was no different. He just doesn't play that way in Super Bowls, he does that in every game."

And so on — Shanahan talking about how proud he was of his team for winning in a hard-fought game, of hanging in and beating a class team and a great organization.

I'll have vanilla.

He is the antithesis of Lombardi; his players rave about him.

"I've seen him get excited . . . but it still looks kind of controlled," said Steve Atwater, the free safety, in a Super Bowl interview. "He's the consummate professional. He's a great leader. I know he has every base covered. Any question you ask him, he can answer."

The Broncos' Tim McKyer, who has played for a bunch of coaches in a bunch of NFL towns, said of Shanahan: "He doesn't even blink. Sure would hate to play Russian roulette with that guy."

Mike Holmgren tried. The Packers' anti-Shanahan scheme was to stuff the Broncos' run offense with their famed defensive linemen — Gilbert Brown, the 345-pounder supposedly immovable defensive tackle, and Reggie White, the All-NFL History defensive end.

Shanahan's offense — Elway passing and running and Davis' running — shredded Holmgren's defenses. The great Reggie White was credited with one tackle. All game.

"We try to establish the run," Shanahan explained in the aftermath. "Most teams that have success in the playoffs and Super Bowl can run the ball."

The cliche corps nodded.

Until he signed his reported $8.5 million contract as head coach of the Broncos, Shanahan was a gypsy football man — a lifer. He is 45 now, was raised in suburban Chicago, played at Eastern Illinois — and was so severely speared in a spring game that his heart stopped beating and he was rendered the last rites of the church. He recovered.

Out of college himself, he made the cross-country campus tour — Oklahoma, Northern Arizona, Minnesota, Florida and on into the pros. Twice as an assistant with the Broncos, head coach for all of 20 games with the Raiders, offensive coordinator with the 49ers. And back to Denver as head coach.

Denver had suffered through 38 seasons without winning an ultimate championship in pro football. And when the Broncos won, their coach snubbed Mickey Mouse.

The Season After

How Super Bowl champions fared the following season:

Season	Winner	Next Year	Results
1966	Green Bay	9-4-1	won Super Bowl II
1967	Green Bay	6-7-1	3rd in NFL Central
1968	New York Jets	10-4	lost playoff opener
1969	Kansas City	7-5-2	2nd in AFC West
1970	Baltimore	10-4	AFC runner-up
1971	Dallas	10-4	NFC runner-up
1972	Miami	12-2	won Super Bowl VIII
1973	Miami	11-3	lost playoff opener
1974	Pittsburgh	12-2	won Super Bowl X
1975	Pittsburgh	10-4	AFC runner-up
1976	Oakland	11-3	AFC runner-up
1977	Dallas	12-4	lost Super Bowl XIII
1978	Pittsburgh	12-4	won Super Bowl XIV
1979	Pittsburgh	9-7	3rd in AFC Central
1980	Oakland	7-9	4th in AFC West
1981	San Francisco	3-6*	tied for 11th in NFC
1982	Washington	14-2	lost Super Bowl XVIII
1983	L.A. Raiders	11-5	lost playoff opener
1984	San Francisco	10-6	lost playoff opener
1985	Chicago	14-2	lost divisional playoff
1986	New York Giants	6-9	last in NFC East
1987	Washington	7-9	3rd in NFC East
1988	San Francisco	14-2	won Super Bowl XXIV
1989	San Francisco	14-2	NFC runner-up
1990	New York Giants	8-8	4th in NFC East
1991	Washington	9-7	lost divisional playoff
1992	Dallas	12-4	won Super Bowl XXVIII
1993	Dallas	12-4	NFC runner-up
1994	San Francisco	11-5	lost divisional playoff
1995	Dallas	10-6	lost divisional playoff
1996	Green Bay	13-3	lost Super Bowl XXXII

*Strike-shortened 1982 season

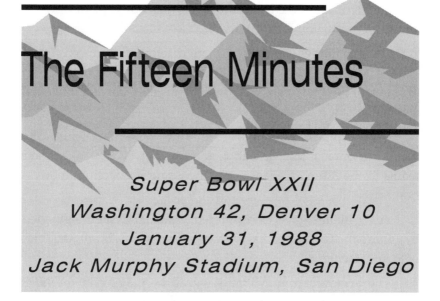

The Fifteen Minutes

Super Bowl XXII
Washington 42, Denver 10
January 31, 1988
Jack Murphy Stadium, San Diego

Perhaps a billion words would be written and read, or spoken and heard, during this wonderful week in advance of Super Bowl XXII. Who can count that high? Maybe more than a billion words as the writers, the TV men, the radio probers crunched and skittered around the athletes who played for the Redskins and the Broncos.

It was picture day in San Diego, a city that Pete Rozelle had discovered and made into a new Super Bowl location. A thousand or so reporters clustered around the Redskins' tall quarterback, Doug Williams, on this photo day. From one of these elite of the world media came a voice that spoke nine words: "Obviously, you've been a black quarterback all your life . . . "

Doug Williams just looked at the person forming this question. *Damn the torpedoes, full-speed ahead. Don't give up the ship. Nuts. Four score and seven years ago. One small step for man, one giant leap for mankind. I have a dream.* Some words, once spoken, are etched in history.

Williams had learned that intellectual capacity in a journalist was never required for the assignment to cover the Super Bowl.

"If you're white, black, yellow or pink, it means a lot to a quarterback if you can take a team to the Super Bowl." Those words had been spoken by Doug Williams.

"Martin Luther King didn't change it, John F. Kennedy didn't change it. All I can do is live my life the way I'm living it and be an example of how you can overcome." Those words, too, had been spoken by Doug Williams.

Doug Williams guided his team to the Super Bowl much the way Joe Montana, Jim McMahon and Phil Simms had taken their teams to the ultimate event — with passing, leadership, motivation and skill.

But Williams gave us a different issue, an issue heightened by Jimmy the Greek and his words — myths, lies, bumbling, bigoted statements.

The Friday before Williams would be playing in the NFC championship game, winner to go to the Super Bowl, the Greek sat down for lunch at Duke Zeibert's restaurant in Washington. A crew from WRC-TV, Washington's NBC outlet, stuck a microphone in the Greek's face. He was asked to say something to commemorate Martin Luther King's birthday. And the Greek spoke, delivering his theories and philosophies for all us TV viewers.

Among other things, he said: ". . . the black is the better athlete, and he practices to be the better athlete, and he's bred to be the better athlete because all this goes way back to the slave period, the slave owner would breed this big black with his big woman so he could have a big black kid. That's where it all started."

He also said: "If they take over the coaching jobs like everybody wants them to, there's not going to be anything left for the white people. I mean, all the players are black. The only thing the whites control is the coaching jobs. Now I'm not being derogatory, but that's all that's left for them. Black talent is beautiful, it's great, it's out there. The only thing left for whites is a couple of coaching jobs."

Suddenly, every network was showing footage of Lunch at Duke's, Noontime with the Greek. The news wires blistered. CBS was appalled. The network had employed the Greek for a dozen years, used his opinions, permitted him to deliver his ass-backwards scoops, provided a forum for him to deliver to us his point spreads.

The Greek apologized. Next day, CBS fired him. The following day Brent Musburger, the Greek's longtime colleague, apologized for CBS. Brent reminded America that the Greek's words did not reflect the thinking or attitudes of the rest of the people at CBS. Thus, pleading itself innocent, CBS permitted the games to go on.

Doug Williams' biography became the story of Super Bowl XXII. As the first black quarterback to start in the event devoted to excess, gluttony, avarice, corporate buffoonery, lechery, sporting pomposity, journalistic incest, Doug Williams' every mouthful was headlines material.

> "Articles say I'm vindictive. They say I have something to prove. I have nothing to prove . . . except to Joe Gibbs and my team."
> — Washington quarterback Doug Williams

"I used to see crosses burning every Friday night," Williams told the writers about his boyhood in Louisiana. "They burned a cross at every intersection. We couldn't go out of the house after dark."

He had lived through hard days — in his boyhood and in his professional manhood.

"Articles say I'm vindictive," Williams said. "They say I have something to prove. I have nothing to prove . . . except to Joe Gibbs and my team."

Gibbs was the only NFL coach to give Williams a decent chance.

Williams had gone to the NFL a decade before Super Bowl XXII. He came out of Grambling, a top-rated quarterback. He was drafted in the first round by the Tampa Bay Buccaneers.

Then, too, he was cast as a man destined to crash through a color barrier. The NFL had never had a premier quarterback whose skin was anything but white. Blacks — James Harris, Joe Gilliam,

John Walton — had played quarterback before in the league, but they were backups mostly, seldom used.

Williams was brought to the NFL to play for a downtrodden expansion team, to lead it in its development, to crumble the myths and the stereotypes. The Bucs, the pro team that had lost its first 24 games, quickly flourished with Williams on the team. Williams was the Bucs' quarterback for five seasons, during which time they went to the playoffs three times. With Williams, the Bucs reached the NFC championship game, the brink of an earlier Super Bowl, but lost.

It was then that the Bucs turned on their quarterback by being cheap in a contract offer. Williams jumped to the USFL, the Oklahoma Outlaws. Then there was the terrible tragedy of the death of Williams' wife, Janice, who died of a brain tumor just after the birth of their daughter, Ashley. Williams went half-crazy. He wondered about life and the cruelty of it.

"I don't think it can get any worse," Williams told the Super Bowl press. "You think, 'why me?' You think about the baby and its mother. You think, 'it should have been me.'"

The USFL went under. Doug Williams, once a No. 1 quarterback in the NFL, was jobless at age 30. It was 1986.

"The only reason I came to this team in Washington is it's the only club that offered me anything," Williams said, "and that as a backup.

"Everybody says that Doug Williams is a better reliever than he is a starter. I've always been a starter.

"For a year I'd been all dressed up and nowhere to go. Go out for the pregame warm-up. Listen to the tunes. Go back to the dressing room. Come back out for the kickoff. Sit on the sidelines.

"Then somebody calls and says, 'hey man, c'mon down here.' You feel wanted."

As successor to Joe Theismann, Jay Schroeder had been a near champion in 1986. Williams was allowed to play and feel wanted in one game, as a reliever. He threw one pass in the '86 season.

At the end of the '86 season, Williams went to Gibbs and asked to be traded to a place where he could play. A trade was fixed with Al Davis and the Raiders: Williams for a second-round draft choice. Then the trade was canceled.

The Redskins started the '87 season with Williams as Schoeder's backup, again. But in the season opener versus the Eagles, Schroeder was injured. Williams rushed in, the emergency quarterback, and threw two touchdown passes. The Redskins won.

The players walked off in another strike in the 1987 season, but this time the NFL did not cut off the games. The NFL hired non-union football players, rejects, the unemployed, camp cuts who become bookkeepers and construction workers, and it played on. The regular players missed only one game day of the season. The NFL counted the games played that day in the season standings.

Mickey Mouse II.

When the strike ended after several games and the genuine football players returned, Williams remained Schroeder's backup. But now there was a pattern. Schroeder would falter, Williams would rush in — and Hail to the Redskins. In the season's final game, Williams came in again and helped save the Redskins from a loss to the Vikings. They produced a 27-24 victory in overtime.

Gibbs changed quarterbacks when the season ended, before the Super Bowl playoffs. Doug Williams was a starter in the NFL for the first time in five years.

Now he was at the Super Bowl in San Diego. He was analyzed, scrutinized, critiqued. Thrust inside a microscope, he was a football player forced to become protagonist in the hottest sociological story of the year.

Williams said it had all started back for him when he bailed out the Redskins in the season opener, when he produced the victory in relief of Schroeder.

"Even Ronald Reagan took a look at that game and said, 'By God, Jesse Jackson will love this,'" said Williams.

◆   ◆   ◆

The truth is the NFL never picked fleabag dumps to put up the elite media corps. A contented scribe is one who would be more inclined to write nice, sweet puff pieces promoting pro football. So went the rationale of Pete Rozelle, whose own origins were in PR.

Now we were in the new shoreside Marriott in San Diego. I had a neat room overlooking the San Diego harbor with its sailboats, ferryboats, great naval ships and flocks of seagulls. It had a stepout porch where I could bask in the afternoon sun after finishing my writing and read the freebie papers and magazines that were dropped in the pressroom to make us happy.

Our own newspapers, of course, had codes of ethics and paid for our hotel rooms and meals. At least, they should have, the days of the total freeload having vanished with the demise of the leather helmet and the single wing.

But every day we had television people interviewing writers, writers interviewing other writers, writers interviewing television people.

My old bugaboo: The media interviewing the media. Nincompoop journalism.

We now had *USA Today* hanging on our hotel room door handles every morning. *USA Today* had created the world in 1982 and discovered the Super Bowl. Anything that might have happened before then did not count, because nothing ever happened before then. The stuff it wrote about was designed to be remembered for 30 seconds, the maximum length of its average reader's memory span.

Mike Lupica, the columnist from New York, was impressed by the writing. "Every story reads like a ransom note."

USA Today's contribution to sporting America was the television column. We learned what Brent Musburger said yesterday when he covered a football game. We learned what Bob Costas said today when *USA Today* discovered that a basketball, along with the planet Earth, was round. We learned what Dick Vitale had to say, in his well-chosen words. And then we learned which team Brent Musburger predicted would win the Super Bowl and why.

A guy named Rudy Martzke assembled all this vital information and published it ransom-note style. He ran the ratings as though they were as important as the scores, and he scared the crap out of all the network bosses lest he write something that showed CBS didn't beat NBC the Sunday when the Cowboys played the Steelers.

◆   ◆   ◆

Bleep John Elway!

Being something of a traditionalist, I went out to the Broncos to hear what John Elway had to say, even though it was against the modern journalistic judgment.

Across John's face was a pair of blue-tinted sun shades. He was chewing gum. This might have been Elton John on tour in Australia, or General Eisenhower on the invasion beach. We — the traditionalists — jostled around him, straining to hear his words. He vanished from my view, from within the elbowing crowd. I squeezed in and craned my neck. I was able to see his white shoes, laces untied, and two white sweat socks. There was a voice, of which one of every four words was audible. I assumed the voice was Elway's.

"Underneath all the hype and hoopla, there's a football game," Elway said.

Somebody moved in and told Elway: "The Top Gun pilots of the U.S. Air Force admired your calm and performance."

"I admire what they do," said Elway. "My job is a lot easier than what they do."

"John," somebody else said, "were your struggles when you were a rookie, years ago, were they humbling?"

"Gee, I didn't know what I was doing," Elway said. "I didn't think it was humbling. I don't think I was an egomaniac when I came into the league. It damaged my confidence. I was shattered. People said my first year I was a bust."

"Were you a bust?" another guy asked.

"Yeah," Elway said.

Somebody — it looked like the guy from Dubuque — chimed in: "The Super Bowl, what is it?"

"The players are sort of sidelights here," said Elway. "It's the media. It's attention. Look at the stories. Most are about the media. It's the spectacle."

The prattle lasted for 45 minutes. Then an NFL PR guy blasted into his power megaphone that the session was history, that Elway was being freed.

"Time flies when you're having fun," said Elway.

"One more question," said a persistent snoop. "The game's in Jack Murphy Stadium. John, do you know who Jack Murphy was?"

"No," said Elway. "No."

"He was a sportswriter," said the sportswriter.

"He must never have written a bad thing to have a stadium named after him," said Elway.

◆　　　◆　　　◆

The bus carried a mob of gringo journalists. It rolled up to the border control south of San Diego, past the barbed wire fences. We rode into Tijuana, in Old Mexico, and stopped on the other side. A Mexican police officer climbed aboard followed by a man in civilian clothes.

"Welcome on behalf of the police department and our mayor to Mexico," the man said. The gringo journalists nodded.

A sign above the street said: Tijuana Welcomes the Super Bowl. The NFL's sanctioned Super Bowl XXII was on the sign. We were hot stuff in Mexico, too.

The bus moved onward, with a police escort. The sirens roared. Here come the gringo Super Bowl media. Mexican urchins stopped, for the moment, offering to peddle their sisters to Yankee tourists. The bus passed through a plaza dominated by a statue of Abraham Lincoln holding a broken chain.

It was the day of the Fiesta de Super Bowl in Tijuana.

The bus deposited us at the Agua Caliente Race Track, and we marched inside. The Tijuana Super Bowl Committee gave us miniature bottles of tequila and gracious smiles and sent us into the clubhouse. The dogs were running. It was shortly after siesta.

Every restaurant in town had set up stands to feed us tortillas, enchiladas, tacos and other Mexican delicacies. The committee told us that the caesar salad was invented in this part of Mexico. And to prove it, right in the Agua Caliente track, they brought in a super bowl, filled it with lettuce and croutons and cheese, and mixed up the world's largest caesar salad. It might have weighed half a ton.

Night came. We were taken to downtown Tijuana. The shops were open, offering their wares to the gringos who write about "Americano Futbol." Ceramic statues, leather bags and switchblade knives were available at bargain rates. The Tijuana cops had closed off Avenida Revelucion, the main drag, for La Fiesta de Super Bowl. Bands played. We wandered down the street, into the Jai-Alai Fronton, where it was Super Bowl night, and back onto the Avenida. The good citizens of Tijuana wondered what was going on.

I jumped on a bus headed back to the San Diego Marriott. The U.S. customs agents at the largest land border crossing in the Western Hemisphere welcomed us home. This is a hot border, and they didn't give a hoot about a busload of American football writers loaded with contraband. They were after illegals.

SAN DIEGO — Joe Gibbs is at his desk at midnight. Sometimes it is difficult to sleep. He breaks out the machine and runs over the films.

Nothing unusual for a coach, viewing the films over and over, looking at familiar figures.

Gibbs, coach of the Redskins, believes a successful football coach must be a workaholic. Monday through Thursday nights, Gibbs sleeps in his office at Redskin Park.

He is being called the best coach in pro football history.

But the late-night films haven't always been of linebackers and running backs. Sometimes Gibbs has watched two lads at play. Throwing footballs. Marching with books in their hands. Not playbooks — school textbooks.

The films are of his two sons. Videotapes of the family from which he separated himself to do his job in his style. His wife, Pat, would operate the video camera at home. The boys, JD and Coy, would perform. Pat would ship the video out to the training facility. Gibbs would watch it on his machine.

This way, Gibbs could compensate for his gnawing conscience.

This is dedication.

He is back at the Super Bowl for the third time in his seventh season with the Redskins. He is here with the team that was not the most talented in its conference. . . .

Diligence pays off. To some, the result justifies neglect of family.

Gibbs had been decreed the top pro football coach of all time in a *Sport* magazine piece just before reaching Super Bowl XXII. Tons of esoteric data were force-fed into a computer by Elias Sports Bureau, official keeper of NFL numbers. Stuff such as improvement or deterioration of teams, how many games the coach won and should have won, how many games he won that he should have lost. The machine spun and whirred and coughed out Gibbs' name as No. 1. The Redskins had won more games than they should have.

Vince Lombardi was second to Gibbs and then came John Madden. Tom Flores was fifth. Don Shula was sixth. Tom Landry, if you could believe it, was 10th.

I disputed this entire notion in a column. Using heart and soul in preference to strange numbers and a computer, I decreed Lombardi tops of all time. And Vince never had to sleep in his office.

◆   ◆   ◆

The Redskins of 1987 were overachievers. That could not be disputed. In this asterisk-pocked season of more Mickey Mouse, they went 11-4. They did a good job of picking strike-breakers when the real guys went out. And Gibbs went against his image as conservative coach when he elected to switch quarterbacks between the finish of the regular season and the playoffs.

It was Doug Williams' time. The Redskins were underdogs when they went into Chicago for the first playoff game. They were quickly down 14-0. Williams brought them back to tie the score and then Washington won it on Darrell Green's 50-yard punt return. The game ended, 21-17, with Walter Payton trying to gain one more yard and being shoved out of bounds. It was his last game, his last play. He had hoped to go back to the Super Bowl for his last hurrah.

With Payton out and Williams in, the Redskins beat the Vikings, 17-14, for the NFC championship. Williams threw two touchdown passes.

◆   ◆   ◆

At La Jolla, where the Broncos were encamped, Dan Reeves spoke to clusters of reporters. Twice Super Bowl losers, beaten badly by the Giants the year before, the Broncos had started to acquire the rank, smelly image of the Minnesota Vikings.

"Our entire football team has been . . . " Reeves paused, searching for the proper word. "Haunted . . . is the word I come up with for last year's loss."

The haunted Broncos had gone through the '87 broken season with a 10-4-1 record. Nobody was more haunted than Karl Mecklenburg, the Teutonic linebacker with the mild persona and the high IQ. He remained tormented by the memory of how the Giants had beaten his team in Super Bowl XXI.

> "A loss is very hard to swallow. I think it's better not to make the playoffs than to lose the Super Bowl."
> — Denver linebacker Karl Mecklenburg

"We learned how to lose a Super Bowl," he said. "Now we have to learn how to win one.

"A loss is very hard to swallow. I think it's better not to make the playoffs than to lose the Super Bowl."

Mecklenburg was surrounded by writers at a table under a tent in La Jolla. One of them told him how the Redskins were changing the numbers of their players at practice. The idea was to confuse any peeping Tom spies.

"Pretty paranoid," said Mecklenburg.

And wasn't it paranoid to say better not make the playoffs at all than to get there and lose the Super Bowl?

The Broncos again rode Elway through the playoffs and back to the Super Bowl. They toyed with the Houston Oilers in their first playoff game. John flipped two touchdown passes and ran for another in a 34-10 victory.

They would be playing the Browns in a rematch of their epic of the year before for the AFC championship. The Browns arrived in Denver with bitter memories and vows of revenge, but all that seemed hollow. Elway took the Broncos to a 21-3 advantage in the first half. In the third quarter, Bernie Kosar fired an 18-yard touchdown pass. Elway fired back with an 80-yarder. Kosar fired back with a 32-yarder.

The rivals were slugging the bejabers out of each other. By the end of the third quarter, the Browns had cut deeply into the Broncos' edge. It was 31-24, Denver, but Kosar was cranking. He produced a 31-31 tie score with another scoring pass early in the fourth. Elway fired back with his third touchdown pass for a 38-31 lead with four minutes left.

The year before, Elway drove the Broncos 98 yards to produce the tie at the end of regulation in the championship game. This year, the ball was Kosar's, and he drove the Browns downfield until they reached the Denver 5. There Kosar handed the ball to Earnest Byner. Byner crashed across the 5, headed for the end zone. Inside the 3, a hand — Jeremiah Castille's — reached out for Byner and stripped the ball away from him. Denver recovered the fumble.

There were 65 seconds left. The Broncos used what they could, then took an automatic safety to save themselves. The final was 38-33. The Browns, torn emotionally, were frustrated again; the Broncos headed to the Super Bowl for the third time.

◆　　　◆　　　◆

A dash of verbal venom is always helpful when it gets dull for us. So it was a joyous occasion when Dexter Manley accused Mike Ditka of possessing the smarts of a grapefruit. This evaluation was offered before the Redskins and the Bears clashed early in the playoffs. It was awarded widespread attention in the football prose written in January. Dexter Manley was one of the most quotable athletes in the league.

Now at the Super Bowl, Dexter Manley, who manhandled quarterbacks for the Redskins, went into his mum act and refused to be interviewed. He was a no-show in the interview tent the NFL set up for the Redskins, lagoon-side, at the Hyatt in San Diego. Dexter's silence became another of those Super Bowl stories that get overkilled.

He actually wasn't hiding. Wandering through the Hyatt's swimming pool area, designed with a pseudo-Polynesian motif, I happened upon Dexter. He was talking with my old friend Moe Siegel, out of Washington. Dexter had some T-shirts with grapefruits on them.

"Did Mike Ditka send you those T-shirts, Dexter?" I asked.

"No," said Manley, "Mike Ditka sent us to the Super Bowl."

He would again be a no-show at the mandatory interview session that day. But he guaranteed his appearance for the next morning, under the tent in San Diego. So it was that he drew a maniacal mob of scribblers and electronitoids to hear his statements, usually directed toward quarterbacks he promised to maim.

Manley arrived late, convoyed by two security guards. He burst through and leaped onto a platform.

Steve Sewell took a reverse from Elway, then threw this halfback pass back to Elway for a 23-yard gain. (Photo©Vernon Biever)

"Ho, ho, ho," said Manley. He had a sheet of paper and appeared to read a statement.

"There are so many questions . . . that in order to save your time and my time I suggest that you submit your questions in writing and I will study them overnight and I will submit my answers tomorrow." He leaped off the platform and left.

We waited. Jilted.

Then minutes later he returned. He was handed the first question in writing. "Why did you come back?"

Manley broke up in giggles. "I'm sweating bullets," he said.

We fired questions.

"I don't need attention," he said. "That's why I wasn't here yesterday. I just like to go out and kick somebody's you know what," he said.

"There comes a point in time you got to take time for yourself," he said. "I sat in my room and meditated. The PR department was upset with me.

"People have a general perception of me," he said. "People make me out to be something I'm not. I'm only a defensive lineman, and you know we're not very smart.

"Why should I be fined for not coming here?" he said. "You got to be a man. You got to have some balls.

"Coach Gibbs had a talk with me," he said. "That's why I came back. When E.F. Hutton talks, you listen.

"I don't want to say some words that get somebody motivated," he said. "Bulletin board stuff. Coach Gibbs is always worried about me saying things. Now he wants me to say things.

"If we don't do the job up front, no question, Denver will be the world champions," he said.

"It's kind of getting kind of boring," he added.

I'd be curious later on, when Dexter Manley went before a Congressional committee and said he'd never learned to read and write. If that were true, how did he read that statement to us?

The papers came out and they were full of Dexter Manley. The San Diego *Tribune* had a long piece on Rudy Martzke and how he was at the Super Bowl, talking to all the TV people and finding out what they were thinking.

We'd reached the Super Bowl ultimate at last — the Martzke Mentality. The media interviewing the media about interviewing the media.

In midweek, the folks at the grandiose Coronado Hotel permitted the media within its hallowed confines when they threw a Super Bowl party just for us. It was a scene out of the '20s for a bunch of guzzling journalists; certainly it ranked in the final four of quality Super Bowl parties. Pete Rozelle's party was pretty good, too. For this one, Pete had obtained use of the Naval Air Station at North Island. This time the only traffic on the runways was the NFL busses and limos for the more elegant.

◆   ◆   ◆

It was a quick haul to Jack Murphy Stadium on the morning of the game. The parking lot was enormous.

The stadium really was named for a sportswriter. Jack Murphy had been a grand writer. He had been a close friend of Red Smith and of Tom Callahan, who wrote splendid sports articles for *Time*. One night, years before, I'd been honored to go to dinner with Jack and Red and Tom at a Super Bowl. The years passed, and now America stopped to watch the Super Bowl. As I walked through the parking lot toward the stadium named in honor of Jack Murphy, I thought of departed friends. Jack had died. Red had died. Jimmy Cannon had died.

Herb Alpert, from the old Tijuana Brass, sang *The Star-Spangled Banner* with the customary pomp. Super Bowl XXII was permitted to begin.

The Redskins were quickly down 10-0. The Broncos, made 3½-point favorites by the oddsmakers still being listened to, scored on their first offensive play. John Elway masterfully fooled Barry Wilburn with an eye fake and enabled Ricky Nattiel, one of his Three Amigos receivers, to go streaking past the defender. In the open field, Nattiel caught the ball from Elway and dashed the distance, 56 yards. It was the fastest touchdown in any of the Super Bowls. On the next possession, Elway turned receiver after a flip to runner Steve Sewell. Sewell's trick-play pass to Elway gained 32 yards against the befuddled Redskins' defense. With the Broncos stopped at the 6, Reeves entrusted Rich Karlis to try a 24-yard

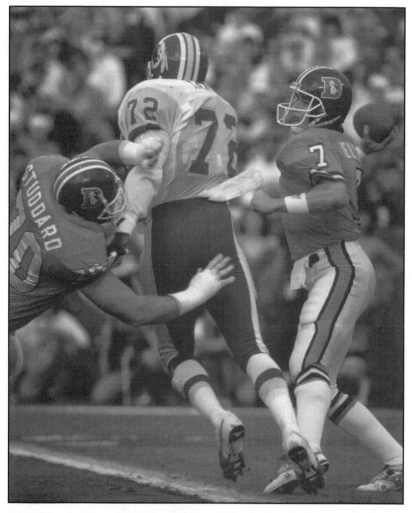

John Elway passes under duress as lineman Dave Stoddard tries to block an onrushing Redskin. (Photo©Vernon Biever)

field goal. Karlis had been haunted for a year by his misses against the Giants. This time he was perfect. The Broncos were threatening to rout the Redskins.

The entire story was blowing up. Williams had four passes dropped in the first quarter. Then he went down in agony. He had been in the midst of his pass retreat when his foot skidded and he fell. The left leg, hooked oddly at the knee, crumpled beneath his body. The right ankle caught and bent in an unnatural direction.

He was hurt, badly. Quarterbacks get damaged in football. All of them. Injury goes with the job. Williams rolled on the grass. He managed to get up, but then he collapsed and was assisted to the bench. Schroeder ran to the huddle. The doctor quickly examined Williams. It was a hyperflexed left knee.

What happened next was history. It was not just a black quarterback playing in the Super Bowl. It was a quarterback performing with exquisite skill, limping, with spasms of pain in his knee. A quarterback winning.

What happened next was the most stunning 15 minutes of the 22 Super Bowls, the most stunning 15 minutes in all the years of pro football. Perhaps the most astounding 15 minutes in all of sports.

"I've played with pain before," Williams told Gibbs at the bench. And Williams went back onto the field to play on his hyperflexed knee.

Williams stepped back gingerly and tossed a short pass designed to gain 7 yards to Ricky Sanders. Sanders got behind the defense and caught the ball and ran off with it, 80 yards for a touchdown. It was 10-7, Denver.

The Redskins got the ball back. Williams moved them downfield. At the 27, he dropped back and passed to Gary Clark, behind the Denver secondary, for his second touchdown. It was 14-10, Washington.

The Redskins got the ball back after Karlis missed, this time on a 43-yard field-goal try. Williams handed off to Timmy Smith on a counter. Smith broke free and ran 58 yards for the third touchdown. It was 21-10, Washington.

The Redskins got the ball back. Williams pumped on a play-action pass and hit Sanders again behind the Broncos. This time it was good for a 50-yard touchdown pass. It was 28-10, Washington, with 3:42 to play in the half.

The Redskins got the ball back on Wilburn's interception of Elway. Williams dropped back to pass and hit Clint Didier for 8 yards and another touchdown. It was 35-10, Washington, with 64 seconds left in the second period.

In these 15 minutes of the second quarter of Super Bowl XXII, Doug Williams produced five touchdowns. He passed for four of them, on plays of 80, 27, 50 and 8 yards. He was 9-for-11 in the quarter for 228 yards. Smith ran for 122 yards on five carries. Sanders caught five passes for 168 yards.

All that on just 18 plays in the quarter. All that in just 15 minutes.

The second half was unnecessary. Pete Rozelle's prime-time Super Bowl became superfluous. Timmy Smith scored another touchdown in the fourth quarter, a 4-yard run. Washington won, 42-10. With another long run of 43 yards, Smith totaled 340 yards, more than Csonka and Franco Harris and Marcus Allen and John Riggins and all the other backs who had run in the Super Bowl.

The Broncos kept coming back to get themselves clubbed. They were now 0-3 in Super Bowls. They'd never even been close. "We know how to get here," said John Elway, "we've got to figure out how to win one."

> "We know how to get here, we've got to figure out how to win one."
> — Denver quarterback John Elway

You bet Doug Williams was history. He was history the way Bart Starr was history. The way Namath and Bradshaw and Griese and Plunkett and Montana and McMahon and Simms were history. Doug Williams, the quarterback who delivered a bravura performance in the ultimate football game, the quarterback who was unwanted by 27 of the 28 clubs when he hunted for a job, was 18-for-29 on this day for 340 yards and those four TDs. Williams outproduced all the others. And when he was mobbed in the locker room he said, simply: "I'm not Jackie Robinson."

Even His Name Says TD

It starts with the talent procurement guys — the scouts with the stopwatches to clock a college athlete's speed in the 40; the guys who become amateur shrinks and figure out what goes on in an athlete's head; the men who can measure a kid's heart.

They are bulky men from the leather-helmet era. They trust their instincts when they evaluate athletes. And then they sit around during the nights at the postseason all-star games and combine tryouts and tell each other how brilliant they are.

The best of them — only the best — start the progression that someday carries on to a championship in the Super Bowl.

Any scout is able to judge the talent of a Barry Sanders. He won a Heisman Trophy in college ball. But then how many Heisman Trophy winners have been flops in the pros?

A sportswriter could figure out that a John Elway would become a brilliant pro after he finished at Stanford.

But the smartest of the scouts work for the best of clubs — and it is this sort of club that sniffs through the lists of available players and plucks a Terrell Davis.

The initials might have provided a hint. For certain, his high school and intercollegiate records provided no indication at all that some day Terrell Davis would be an MVP in a Super Bowl.

But here is the raw data: 1,750 yards rushing during the 1997 season; two TDs and 184 yards against the Jaguars in the Broncos' wild-card playoff; two Tds and 101 yards against the Chiefs in the divisional playoff; one TD and 139 yards against the Steelers in

the AFC championship game.

And three Tds and 157 yards against the Packers in Super Bowl XXXII.

Eight touchdowns — eight salutes in the end zone by Davis — in the postseason.

Salutes to the Broncos' talent procurement group for discovering the athlete registered as 6-b in their 1995 draft. That's it, 6-b, signifying Denver's second selection in that sixth round.

Before Davis, the NFL clubs — all with wise, know-everything scouts — drafted 195 other players. The clubs would go through round after round, Davis so down on his own prospects that he did not even bother to watch the draft out of curiosity on TV. Nineteen other running backs were drafted before TD's name came up.

"I was surprised to even have been drafted because in college I didn't even have the stats," Davis said during the Super Bowl hype period. "I figured I was going to be a free agent. Funny, the team that I talked to most, both at the combine and over the phone, was the Packers."

Davis, No. 196, would develop the most famous headache in sports history — and score the winning touchdown in the second-most shocking upset of the XXXII Super Bowls. Only Joe Namath's Jets at Super Bowl III had been larger underdogs than the Broncos, against whom the odds were 11 1/2 points at kickoff time of SB XXXII.

Even in his boyhood fantasies, Davis never calculated that he was destined for such stardom. After he had been drafted, No. 196 did not waste time on grandiose thoughts.

"Something told me I could play the game, but I thought if I was going to make it at this level, I was going to be a backup," he told the media during Super Bowl week. "That first year, I was banking on just making the practice squad."

Yet there he was in his hometown, San Diego, where he had skipped football until his junior year in high school at Lincoln Prep. There in San Diego, he was cornered by the jokers and clowns who flock to Media Day, posing questions about trees and shrubs. There he was the AFC's rushing champion — Elway's choice for the best running back in football.

"I was a nerd with a backpack," he told Super Bowl interviewers about his high school period. "I wasn't even a good nerd. I had a backpack full of F's in it.

"I was kind of rebellious at that time. I got bad grades. I even flunked P.E. I had P.E. sixth period, and I used to leave after fifth period and go home."

Even so after his lackluster career at Lincoln, he was taken into a college program. George Allen always had a knowledge of talent, and he never paid much heed to background. He recruited Davis for Long Beach State, his last coaching location. Still, the old NFL coach, a Super Bowl loser with the Redskins, violated is own credo — The Future Is Now. Allen redshirted Davis as a freshman.

"I was on the Scout Team, and he used to call me Secretariat," Davis said at the Super Bowl. "He was probably one of the first people who recognized that I was a pretty good back."

The Long Beach State program was so strapped, Davis and his teammates were required to pay for their own football cleats. Then Allen died. Long Beach State soon gave up football.

Davis transferred across the continent to Georgia. There he was snubbed by Ray Goss, the head coach. Once at Georgia, Davis wasn't even permitted to stand on the sidelines during a game for which he was not in uniform. He was refused a sideline pass.

When he was in uniform, Davis never dazzled at Georgia.

Gary Kubiak heard of him through the grapevine — from a college coaching friend. Kubiak had been Elway's backup at one time, long enough to stand at the sidelines during three losing Super Bowls. Kubiak, by 1995, had advanced to offensive coordinator on Mike Shanahan's new staff.

Davis was recommended and projected as a third-round draft possibility. Then the Broncos passed on him through several rounds themselves.

At his first training camp, in Greeley, Colorado, Davis was so impressive on special teams and in the second backfield that Shanahan promoted him to starter. Davis ran for 1,117 yards as a rookie runner.

It would be a while before Davis developed his personal touchdown celebration. The end zone spike is out. The salute is in.

On each TD, Davis snapped to attention in the end zone and raised his right arm in a polished salute to his teammates. Sort of like Bill Clinton to the Marine guard when he steps off the presidential helicopter.

"That's our mentality, a soldier mentality," Davis explained to the curious Super Bowl media. "There's a rapper, Master P. He has a song, 'No Limit Soldier.'

"We thought that theme would fit well with us."

So it was Davis snapped back from his migraine against the Packers and rendered three TD salutes.

And afterwards, he told the press:

"This is like a dream. I'm kind of numb. It almost never happened to me. In the second quarter, I really couldn't see straight.

"I was dinged and knew I had a migraine coming on. But I also knew there was a good chance that it would go away. . .

"In bed last night I thought about playing well and knowing that I had to play well."

Three times in losing Super Bowls it was pretty much John Elway's arm and feet against the enemy. He didn't have much ground support.

At this Super Bowl he did. So, across the press interview tent, there was one more salute:

"In my book he's the best running back in the league bar none," said John Elway. "He's always breaking tackles and he's always going north and south."

(Author's message for John Elway — TD was terrific, he has been for three years, he now has a ring and an MVP award and endorsements and the adoration of all of Denver. But John, this is my book, and truthfully not just because I'm from Detroit, but . . .)

A Loudmouth
Bleeping Linebacker

Once upon a time a linebacker named Jack Lambert went on Monday Night Football to converse with Howard Cosell. Lambert proceeded to suggest that if the NFL did not want its quarterbacks touched by rushing hands the league should put them in pantyhose and paint them with lipstick and rouge.

"If they don't want quarterbacks to get hit they should put them all in dresses," were Lambert's exact words.

He got fined.

He also got an overflowing mailbag.

"I got a lot of trouble," Lambert said at Super Bowl XIII. "A lot of hate mail from women libbers. They called me a male chauvinist. They said my mother should be ashamed of me."

Lambert said all this with red-rimmed eyes behind black-lensed glasses, from whatever activities he had participated in the evening before.

A couple of tables away Mean Joe Greene said: "Jack Lambert is so tough that he doesn't like himself."

This is all pertinent because the notorious Bill Romanowski listed Jack Lambert as his favorite football player when he was growing up.

"He was one of my idols," Romanowski said when he was mobbed by Super Bowl journalists probing to discover what makes him tick.

"I loved the way he played. I loved his intensity."

He was mobbed because a few weeks earlier he had spit into the face of J.J. Stokes in the game against the 49ers. Romanowski had played most of his career with the 49ers and played in two winning Super Bowls. The spitting incident happened to be in a Monday Night game and happened to be caught on camera by ABC's eagle-eyed video cameramen. ABC's erudite program director played and replayed the incident — doing everything but showing it in slow motion so America could see the wad of spittle dripping through the air.

Of course, there was outrage. Moral outrage. Racial outrage. Media outrage.

The NFL fined Romanowski $7,500. Two his teammates, Shannon Sharpe and Willie Green said if a black player had spit into the face of a white player, the fine would have been stiffer. They were probably right.

With the Broncos threatened with dissension along racial lines, coach Mike Shanahan called a meeting.

"If you just read the headlines in the newspaper, it was a racial problem," Shanahan said during one of his Super Bowl media sessions. "And it wasn't a racial problem. What we did was talk about what was in the article. Everybody expressed their opinions. Everybody got it off their chests."

Romanowski stood and apologized.

But as happens when some such incident occurs, we the media pound it over and over, and twist it around. TV shows the clip again, then again — and 50 times again, repetitiously. The video tape never wears out.

So it was Romanowski was hit on by the media every day during Super Bowl week.

"The guys had their opinions and they expressed their opinions," Romanowski said. "If it would have been one of my teammates I probably would have expressed an opinion, too. The bottom line is my teammates respect me. They know I made a mistake.

"I said I was sorry, and that is that. I did what I did. I said I was sorry."

After all, Romanowski is a linebacker who used to punch up on Jerry Rice at practice during his years with the 49ers. Rice, the untouchable.

But his behavior stems simply from the special mentality required to play linebacker. Joe Schmidt, first of the great lineback-

69

ers had it, during the Lions' championship seasons in the 1950s. Ray Nitschke during the Packers' championship seasons of the 1960s had it. Dick Butkus had it. He used to watch the movie scene in which Richard Widmark rolled the old lady down a flight of stairs in her wheelchair. "I kind of liked that," Butkus said once in a TV interview. Mike Lucci, when he played for the Lions, referred to himself as "a loudmouth bleeping linebacker."

Lambert, obviously, was motivated to fury on the field by that special mentality. Chris Spielman has it.

And for sure, Bill Romanowski has it.

A New Englander, Romanowski played at Boston College on a team with Doug Flutie. He was drafted by the 49ers in 1988. He fit in, part of a team. The 49ers won the Super Bowl Romanowski's first two seasons. He was part of the 49ers' crushing of the Broncos in the 55-10 game at Super Bowl XXIII. It was the year Matt Millen, another with the linebacker mentality, stuck his tongue out at John Elway in midgame.

When Romanowski joined the 49ers, Bill Walsh, the coach; Joe Montana, the quarterback; and Jerry Rice, the wide receiver were the newsmakers on the team.

Romanowski soon became the noisemaker.

A couple of times, he nailed Rice on reverse plays during training camp scrimmages. Rice one time retaliated with a punch. Romanowski punched back at the forbidden target. The 49ers' entire offensive line attacked him — his teammates.

"Guys who know me know the way I am," Romanowski said in a pre-Super Bowl interview, going over the Stokes spitting incident. "They know I don't see color. They know I'll fight anybody. I didn't see a black man in my face.

"But I used to get into fights with Rice in training camp and people wrote me letters saying I'd fight only black guys."

It is not quite true.

During the '97 preseason, Romanowski nailed Carolina quarterback Kerry Collins, helmet to helmet. Collins was sent out, never really to regain his touch during the entire season. The league fined Romanowski $20,000.

Romanowski played six seasons with the 49ers. In 1994, as the 49ers were rebuilding for another Super Bowl victory, Romanowski was traded to the Eagles for two middling draft choices. He played two seasons in Philadelphia. Then in 1996, he exiled himself to Denver as a free agent. That year, he was voted to the Pro Bowl for the first time.

It is, of course, coincidental, but the spitting incident could be construed as the catalyst that drove the Broncos to the Super Bowl. They had lost to Pittsburgh and would lose to San Francisco on that Monday night. But then they had their bittersweet meeting. After

that, they defeated the Chargers in their final game, and as a wild card, they rolled onward to the Super Bowl and ultimate victory.

"All the focus went to me," Romanowski said pre-Super Bowl to the media, "and everyone else could concentrate on football. It was stupid and it was wrong and I held myself accountable.

"Bottom line is, we did turn things around."

It the very late minutes of Super Bowl XXXII Romanowski made a vital play — perhaps the most vital defensive play by Denver the entire game. He nailed Dorsey Levens for no gain in the Packers' drive in the last moments. And he made the most visible play, taking a swing at Mark Chmura that America and the world saw on TV — and the officials in their striped shirts somehow missed.

"That's all part of the game within the game," said Romanowski in the aftermath. "One time they caught me swinging at him on camera, but that's what happens in the heat of battle."

After he spoke to Will McDonough in NBC's swansong Super Bowl interview — the one in which he said the Packers buildup made him want to puke — Romanowski hit the media interview tent. He stood there as long as media folk would ask him questions. He wore a Super Bowl XXXII champions cap — and his uniform was very dirty.

"Nobody gave us a chance," he said. "But we knew in our hearts that we were the best team. Our offensive line just dominated their defensive line. We went out and showed the world we're the best team.

"We were tired of telling Green Bay how good they were during the two weeks of media sessions, and we finally got to go out there and show everybody what we could do."

Just another loudmouth bleeping linebacker!

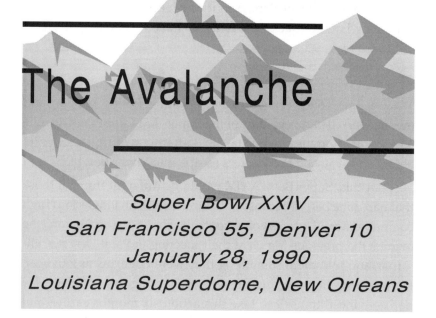

The Avalanche

Super Bowl XXIV
San Francisco 55, Denver 10
January 28, 1990
Louisiana Superdome, New Orleans

John Elway came into pro football with a reverie. Celebrated, fought over, flushed with a media overkill before he ever launched his first forward pass in the NFL, Elway fancied himself as Terry Bradshaw reincarnate.

"My goal is to beat Terry Bradshaw," Elway had once said, listing his ambitions. "He won the Super Bowl four times. I want to win it five."

Now, in January 1990, Elway was a double loser, 0-and-2 in Super Bowls. Instead of being another Terry Bradshaw, Elway was in dreaded danger of becoming another Francis Tarkenton, the three-time Super Bowl loser quarterback. The Broncos did not remind America of the Pittsburgh Steelers in character. They had the odor of the Minnesota Vikings about them.

"We know how to get here," said Elway. "But we got to figure out how to win one."

Beaten, humiliated, in three Super Bowls, the Broncos were back at Super Bowl XXIV in New Orleans. The 49ers were back, too, victors in three Super Bowls in eight seasons with the opportunity to match the Steelers. And it was Joe Montana, 3-and-0 as a Super Bowl quarterback, who had the chance of equaling the feats of Bradshaw.

◆   ◆   ◆

Harping, controversy, barking, bickering, rioting, pushing and media overkill had been part of the Super Bowl since Pete Rozelle had squatted on the sideline late that afternoon in Dallas 23 years before and watched the Packers escape into Super Bowl I.

But this, Super Bowl XXIV, would be different from all those that had gone before because Pete Rozelle was no longer lord high commissioner of professional football. He had stood before the owners the previous March at their meeting in Palm Desert, California, and told them something they were not expecting to hear. He was resigning, leaving the NFL, delivering the self-ziggy. He had convinced himself to take this action six months earlier, and he had kept his secret from leaking. The owners were rocked. The media were shocked.

Rozelle had come in as commissioner of the NFL with clean hands in 1960. History had captured that era with one word: Camelot. John F. Kennedy, a former Harvard receiver, would defeat Richard Nixon, a self-styled play caller for pro coaches, in a major matchup for the presidency later that year. The Super Bowl had not yet been concocted. America had not yet become divided by a war in Vietnam. The Beatles were still juveniles living in Liverpool blight.

Pete would be commissioner for 29 years. During his years, pro football soared in popularity, in wealth, in size, in shape. He cajoled the TV networks; he fought a war and handled a merger; he was attacked by some of the owners, Al Davis and others; he was mocked on occasion by the media; he was faulted, at times, by the players and their association; he was grilled in Congress; he created the most-watched, most successful sporting enterprise in America.

Now Pete Rozelle would be another slice of history. What he constructed in pro football had been imitated by the other pro sports, all envious at the marketing acumen and appeal of the NFL. Rozelle was the best commissioner who ever lived, who ever bossed any sport. And now he wanted to sniff the daisies while he still was able, at age 63.

"I won't miss the power," Rozelle told me when I went to New York to interview him in his office overlooking Park Avenue two months after the Palm Desert proclamation. "I'll miss the action. So much has happened in the last 29 and a half years. It's been exciting to be part of the growth. But I won't miss the power. I'll miss the Super Bowl Sunday."

We were seated near the window. The sun was streaming through. I asked Pete how he would like to be remembered.

"That I did my best," he said. "I was fair. A lot of owners have written me to that effect . . . and that I was part of the great growth of the National Football League. This was a very exciting period."

The owners procrastinated in determining Rozelle's successor. Jim Finks, the president of the New Orleans club, almost made it. But then some of the newer club owners rebelled. There was battling, fighting and trashing. Once again, a compromise man was needed. That's how Pete Rozelle, 29 years earlier, had been selected commissioner.

The owners eventually settled on Paul Tagliabue as their new commissioner. Tagliabue had been the league's attorney. He had been a basketball player at Georgetown. And he would be at Super Bowl XXIV as a curiosity, as the man elected to follow the master, a man, perhaps, with some new ideas.

From now on, the Friday night parties before the Super Bowls would be Paul Tagliabue's parties. Pete Rozelle had a standing invitation to them.

There would be one more dramatic change at this Super Bowl XXIV: Bill Walsh was not coach of the 49ers anymore. Eddie DeBartolo's gut feeling the previous January had been more than just that. Super Bowl XXIII and the 49ers' last-minute victory were Walsh's last hurrah. He went to work as an analyst for NBC, a genius in the booth.

Super Bowl XXIV was the first for new NFL commissioner Paul Tagliabue. Here he appears before the media during Super Bowl week for the first time.

George Seifert, Walsh's defensive expert, was promoted to the head coaching job. So there would be a rookie head coach at Super Bowl XXIV.

◆　　◆　　◆

The New Orleans hospitality folks had busses at the airport to meet the invading reporters. Riding into town, the hostess spoke to us in pure New Orleans.

"There's a *pahty* tomorra night, and anooother *pahty* Fri-dee. . . ." Then we were handed doubloons, coins minted for flipping into the crowds at Mardi Gras. The doubloons could be exchanged for three beignets, which are globs of dough covered with powdered sugar and considered a New Orleans delicacy.

The hostess went into a spiel about the virtues of New Orleans. By then we were tooling outside the airport, and I spotted my first Super Bowl balloon. It bobbed and floated, sort of like

John Madden. It was a Miller Lite balloon, and it was rigged to the roof of a roadside shack belonging to A&L Auto Supply.

The Super Bowl had become a war of beers as well as football teams. Miller had the NFL man of the year. Budweiser had its Bud Bowl. We were supposed to be pitchmen now.

◆   ◆   ◆

The Super Bowl had become so hot that the sportswriters and the guys with the electronic gizmos could no longer repress their anxieties until the scheduled media day on Tuesday morning. Press conferences were arranged for Monday evening. The NFL media men conscripted the Broncos for a pre-media day press conference under a huge tent on the parking lot of the Intercontinental Hotel. Something like 47 TV trucks were parked outside. Each had thick cable wires taped onto the sidewalk from the street into the big top. Lights blazed.

Dan Reeves, the Denver coach, spoke. He was at his eighth Super Bowl, as player and coach. Most of his appearances were losses.

> "We realize the task in front of us. We're reminded of it every day by the press who tell us we don't have a chance."
>
> — Denver coach Dan Reeves

"I do believe in the law of averages," Reeves said. "And hopefully, if I'm here long enough, the law of averages will catch up, and I'll win.

"We realize the task in front of us. We're reminded of it every day by the press who tell us we don't have a chance."

◆   ◆   ◆

It was New Orleans and dinner time. We went off to a place called the Old N'awlins Cookery and ate dinner in a courtyard and talked about football. The conversation was mostly about Elway and Montana, and the fact that the 49ers already were 12½-point favorites and the spread was getting larger.

"Remember Super Bowl III," I cautioned, digging back into my history. "Joe Namath." The other writers scoffed.

We all walked back to the hotel, the Hyatt. I stopped off in the pressroom, by habit. There were always all sorts of goodies there for the media — canvas bags with advertising, football magazines, newspapers, city tour tips. They had something new for us this time — free packets of Bayer aspirin. Years ago, I might have wanted it.

◆　　◆　　◆

It was media day, and we'd marched across the bridge from the Hyatt. John Elway was the picture of the nonchalant hero, his audience of hundreds at his feet. Those dancing feet were up on a railing in front of the first row of the Superdome grandstands. He cupped his hands on his blond head. His voice was husky.

John floated in the fishbowl atmosphere. He lived in it. The previous Halloween a couple of reporters from Denver's *Rocky Mountain News* bundled up their kids in costume and rang the bell at Elway's house. Trick or treat. John gave the kids treats. He handed out Reese's Peanut Butter Cups and KitKat bars.

It was trick.

The reporters wrote in their paper what John Elway gave away for Halloween. It so happened Elway was being paid to endorse Nestle's Crunch bars.

> *"For me to be the quarterback I want to be, we've got to win this game. I've been twice and haven't won."*
> — *Denver quarterback John Elway*

A few days later, Elway told *Sports Illustrated* that he was about to suffocate — his word — as quarterback in Denver.

Now he was suffocating at the usual Super Bowl interview with the mob jostling below him. "There's pressure in every game," he said, "so there's no more for me in this.

"Any time your team's been to the Super Bowl three times and lost, and this is your fourth time, there's a little bit of a monkey. You win, and you lose that monkey. You can be 1-and-8, and you don't have that monkey on your back like 0-and-4.

"For me to be the quarterback I want to be, we've got to win this game. I've been twice and haven't won.

"If we win, it'll be the greatest upset of all time."

I managed to squeeze and push into the second rank below Elway. "You want to guarantee it?" I piped up.

Elway grinned.

"Get us another point and a half, and I'll guarantee it," said John Elway.

He pondered.

"I guarantee we'll cover the spread," he said.

A bit later I stood on a line of about a million sportswriters and electronic media marvels. We were beneath the Superdome, watched over by the yellow-jacketed NFL security to make sure we didn't misbehave. We were awaiting the NFL-catered breakfast that would cause my cholesterol level to soar.

I returned to the field after breakfast. The NFL already had the game clock running on the scoreboard, the countdown to the moment when the 49ers would be trooped out to meet the media.

Bubba Paris, weight listed at 299 pounds but looking heavier, lugged out his camcorder and seated himself on the platform. A female reporter started to question Paris about his weight.

"I'm going to interview you," said Paris, pointing his zoom lens down at her. "How does it feel to know that you have to go someplace and ask a person the only question that aggravates him?"

The reporter persisted. "Why do you have to lose weight if you're playing so well?"

"I can't fit in Porsches, and my kids don't have anything to eat," said Paris, not softly. "I'm eating their food. You got any more questions?"

"I'm too embarrassed to go on," said the reporter. "I'm going to leave now."

She walked away. "See, I'm not fat," said Paris. "I'm big."

I walked back to the Hyatt and went to the front desk. A TV crew from Sacramento came to the desk. The little red light went on. The camera whirred. I was a prop, making believe I was registering at the press hotel. At Super Bowl XXIV, I'd become vital news at six in Sacramento.

◆   ◆   ◆

That afternoon there was a press conference for Bud Bowl II. This scripted game between animated bottles of beer, butting into each other like jocks, would be contested during commercial breaks of Super Bowl XXIV. Bud Bowl I presumably had been worth the expense. So we were going to have Bud versus Bud Light again, with honest-to-goodness TV announcers. Budweiser introduced Brent Musburger and Terry Bradshaw as the men who would describe and analyze the bottle-butting during the breaks when America used to go to the bathroom on Super Sunday.

Terry had learned to spell TV among his readin' and learnin' accomplishments. He had graduated to CBS, as a thinking head. Now the writers at the press conference wondered about Terry's opinions of John Elway.

"I think John's problem is he's been babied by the fans, the media, and, to an extent, by the coaches," Bradshaw said. "It's really too easy for him."

> *"Is he a great quarterback? Nope. A good one. When you choose a profession, and if you don't reach a pinnacle, you can't consider yourself a success."*
> *— former Pittsburgh quarterback Terry Bradshaw on John Elway*

Bradshaw mentioned that Elway was 0-and-2 in Super Bowls and was about to be 0-and-3.

". . . he's too inconsistent. He lets too many things bother him. He's got to get a little tougher emotionally. Things like that shouldn't bother you when you're making two million dollars a year."

This was better stuff than promotional piffle about Bud against Bud Light.

"Is he a great quarterback?" said Bradshaw. "Nope. A good one. When you choose a profession, and if you don't reach a pinnacle, you can't consider yourself a success."

There was one standard of greatness to Bradshaw: Super Bowl rings. John Elway, the man who'd wished for five, had none.

◆   ◆   ◆

I called J.P. McCarthy back at WJR in Detroit early every morning to talk Super Bowl on his radio show. We discussed the scene. The NFL was upset by the scalping of hotel rooms in New Orleans. The problem was, the NFL coppers said, rooms that sold for 125 bucks a night, plus tax, were being reserved and paid for, then sublet via travel agents for 400 or more a pop.

J.P. told me the wires were full of stories that the London bookies, with the 49ers huge favorites, were taking British action on the coin toss and on who'd flub the first field goal.

He asked about Bourbon Street. I made it there one night. I walked into The Old Absinthe House through one door and surveyed the crowd. I didn't know anybody. I left through another door and walked back to the Hyatt. I had to be up early to go on the radio before going to the 49ers.

"I used to go to bed at 4 a.m. at the Super Bowl," I told the listeners back in Detroit. "Now I wake up at 4 a.m."

◆   ◆   ◆

A few days after the 49ers won Super Bowl XXIII, George Seifert boarded a plane in San Francisco. He was going to Cleveland, but he was unable to get a direct flight and had to change planes in Dallas. Seifert had been Bill Walsh's longtime defensive coordinator. Now he was going to Cleveland to be interviewed for the head coaching job of the Browns, which had been vacated when Marty Schottenheimer had been pushed out.

Seifert had dreamed of being a head coach in the NFL, as Bill Walsh had dreamed in the 1970s. Seifert's roots were with the 49ers. As a boy, in the 49ers' early seasons, Seifert was an usher on Sundays at Kezar Stadium. He went to Utah and majored in zoology and played football in the non-glamour positions of offensive guard and linebacker. Then he went into college coaching and got a head coaching job at Cornell. It was Ivy League football, no pressure, no alumni pounding. Right. His teams won three games in three years and Seifert was fired.

He then took an assistant's job at Stanford, where his boss was Bill Walsh, the NFL coach-in-waiting. When the 49ers, at last, summoned Walsh, Seifert rode up with him.

Because of what had happened at Cornell, Seifert didn't seek another head coaching job for many years. He had lost his confidence. And then, in the last week of January 1989, he was aboard the airplane headed for Cleveland. He landed in Dallas and looked at the board to find the gate of his connection.

He went to a pay phone and called home. There was a message to call the office back in San Francisco. Walsh had quit. Eddie DeBartolo was offering George Seifert the 49ers' head coaching job, the opportunity to succeed Bill Walsh, the genius.

Seifert called Cleveland, apologized, and caught the next plane back to San Francisco.

Now he stood before a ballroom full of curious media people at the Hilton near the Mississippi River in downtown New Orleans. Seifert had gray hair, and he wore wire-rimmed eyeglasses. He looked professorial.

He spoke. He charmed us with the best fish story since Hemingway.

He was fishing, he said, off the California coast in the Pacific. His hook caught, and he brought in his catch. He heaved it into his boat. He was happy. He figured it weighed 27 pounds.

Then he realized the boat was taking on water. He started rowing toward the shoreline. The boat was sinking and he had to abandon it. He tried to save the fish, as Hemingway's fisherman had. Seifert went into the drink, holding the fish. He tried to swim with it, but he had to let go.

"That was the biggest striped bass I ever caught," Seifert told us. "I hated to give it up, but my pants were filling up with water."

Seifert told us he'd returned to the spot where he'd surrendered his fish.

"I still enjoy being on the edge," he said. "I like to gamble a little. I've returned to the scene. Like if you're in a trampoline accident, if you fall off, you get back on.

"And I did that some in football."

◆　　◆　　◆

I jammed into the first of the week's media parties, in a tent between the hotel and the Superdome. N'awlins jazz ricocheted through the tent. They stuffed us with gumbo and beef.

I pushed through the mob and encountered the folks from Denver, faithful still. One guy was stuffed into an orange metal barrel, which was held up by suspenders. His gut rolled over the top. He looked as if he were otherwise stark naked, except for the orange cowboy hat on his head.

To pump the card show in the adjoining tent, each media person was given a packet of Super Bowl cards. I roamed into the next tent to look at the football and baseball cards and magazines assembled by the traders and collectors. I was offered eight bucks for my packet of free Super Bowl cards. I rejected it. Somebody else offered 10 bucks. I rejected that, too. Later, the price was raised to 25. I kept mine.

> *"Terry Bradshaw has been bashing me since I got in the league. He didn't like the money I make. He still doesn't. He can stick it in his ear."*
> *— Denver quarterback John Elway*

In the interview tent at the Intercontinental, John Elway responded to Terry Bradshaw. "Terry Bradshaw has been bashing me since I got in the league. He didn't like the money I make. He still doesn't. He can stick it in his ear."

Dan Reeves responded: "I played against Terry Bradshaw, and John Elway is as tough as Terry Bradshaw ever was. Terry Bradshaw had a hell of a supporting cast, and he better be thankful for that."

Overnight, the Bradshaw-Elway controversy dwindled to zero. In Washington, television station WJLA hit the air with a report that three quarterbacks, all white, had tested positive for high levels of cocaine usage. No names were mentioned. But the NFL was charged with a coverup, with racism and with playing favorites. On the air, the station questioned the competence of the testing laboratory operated by Dr. Forest S. Tenant, the NFL's drug adviser.

Because the station had not identified the three supposed users, rumors spread through New Orleans. Reporters chased around, whispering, mentioning station WJLA and the reporter who had gone on the air with the piece, Roberta Baskin. She had said the three quarterbacks or their agents had confirmed the allegations. Ted Koppel discussed the report on the ABC network.

The station had obviously sat on the story until Super Bowl week. Then, it could make the heaviest impact, catch the most notoriety for the station.

The standards of professional journalism decreed that this station identify the quarterbacks it accused. Otherwise, every white quarterback in the league was suspect. Otherwise, the news value was reduced to innuendo and common gossip. No names, no story.

One name mentioned in the subsequent rumor-mongering was Joe Montana. "Did you ever fail a drug test?" Montana was asked on ESPN.

"No, only an accounting test," said Joe.

Joe Browne denied the story for the NFL, denied that the league played favorites, and said the station was on a witch hunt.

None of the Super Bowl reporters could confirm the Washington TV story. But as Ted Koppel said, the drug story had altered the Super Bowl's focus, just as the unsubstantiated TV gambling accusations against Lenny Dawson had altered the focus 20 years earlier at Super Bowl IV, just as a TV reporter's imagination altered the focus when he thought he heard somebody say that Jim McMahon had referred to New Orleans womanhood as sluts.

◆　　◆　　◆

When Vince Lombardi gave up coaching in Green Bay after winning the first two Super Bowls, he was replaced by Phil Bengtson. Bengtson had devised the defense that turned Super Bowl I, that enabled Lombardi to flip the football in the Packers' locker room and preen about the NFL's superiority in running with it and catching it. The Packers had flopped all over Bengtson once he replaced Lombardi.

The most difficult job in coaching sports might be to follow the man who has built and led a dynasty. The footsteps mentality. They are almost always too huge.

"On the contrary," said Seifert at Super Bowl XXIV when asked whether he wanted to deliver his own impact after he replaced Walsh. "It was a matter of continuity. Keeping what Walsh left here."

With Joe Montana and Jerry Rice and Roger Craig and Ronnie Lott — plus the addition of Matt Millen, who was cast off by Al Davis and the Raiders — the 49ers steamrollered through their season. They finished at 14-2, the best record in the league. They entered the playoffs powerful, dominant.

Montana threw four touchdown passes in the first playoff game against the Vikings, completing 17 of 24 for the day. The 49ers won, 41-13. The next weekend they won their fourth NFC championship of the decade by devouring the Rams, 30-3. Montana threw two touchdown passes. He completed 26 of 30.

Continuity! The 49ers were better than ever as they hit their fourth Super Bowl in eight years, their first with George Seifert.

Bill Walsh, certified genius that he was, had never beaten the Broncos in four meetings while he was a coach.

◆　　◆　　◆

Dan Reeves took the Broncos into the Superdome for practice Thursday. Looking around, he noticed that they had painted all the previous Super Bowl scores on the rim of the mezzanine. Winning teams' helmets first, to the left side, losers' to the right.

"They had Super Bowl XXIV up there with the place for the scores blank," said Reeves, "and they already had a San Francisco helmet painted on the left and a Denver helmet painted on the right. They expect us to lose.

"We're going to do our damnedest to make them change it."

There was cause for paranoia for Denver.

The Broncos could handle the AFC well enough, playing well in the season and winning four conference championships, three of these in four years.

But . . . with Elway excelling, with Bobby Humphrey providing strong running as a rookie, the Broncos went 11-5 during the season. Again, it was the best record in the conference entering the playoffs.

In the first playoff game, the Broncos were behind the Steelers through most of the game, but Elway rallied them twice. The second time he took them on another long drive, 71 yards, to a touchdown with less than 2½ minutes to play. The Broncos survived, 24-23.

The next week, the Browns, now coached by Bud Carson, were the Broncos' opponents in the AFC championship game. For the third time in four years, the two clubs bashed each other, first the Broncos, then the Browns rallying. Elway drove the Broncos 80 yards for a decisive touchdown in the fourth quarter. The Broncos won it again, 37-21 — and pity the Browns and Art Modell.

◆　　◆　　◆

Super Bowls make for gleeful owners. As the Broncos geared for the Super Bowl before leaving Denver, their owner, Pat Bowlen, took some swats at the 49ers.

"Those guys have got a great owner," he said. "They got God for a quarterback. They got a Chinaman who plays wide receiver whose feet never touch the ground."

Huh? said the Denver guys.

"That Chinese guy," said Bowlen. "What's his name? Rice?"

The Broncos' PR guy

> *"We're just a bunch of Palookas from the mountains who wear funny uniforms. So maybe we've got a chance. We're going to sneak up on them."*
> — *Denver owner Pat Bowlen*

had to explain that Bowlen was just playing on words, that, hey, this was no ethnic slur.

"We're just a bunch of Palookas from the mountains who wear funny uniforms," said Bowlen. "So maybe we've got a chance. We're going to sneak up on them."

John Madden now had his own Super Bowl TV special.

"There's one word to describe them," Madden said, speaking of the 49ers. "Efficient.

"You go in their locker room, and it doesn't even stink."

◆　◆　◆

I heard a good story. In 1988, when Bill Walsh benched Joe Montana, Eddie DeBartolo had traded his quarterback plus a first draft choice for Billy Ray Smith. It was a done deal, but the Chargers backed up, and the 49ers were stuck with Joe Montana.

As I waited for the glass capsule elevator on the 18th floor of the Hyatt, I spotted the visiting Pete Rozelle. I walked over to greet him, and he introduced me to the man with him, Paul Tagliabue.

Tagliabue held his first Super Bowl press conference Friday at noon in an overflowing ballroom. The focus was on the drug story. This would be the first battle-testing of the new commissioner.

He went for the issue.

"A smear and a gross distortion," Tagliabue said. "It is a journalistic Molotov cocktail. It takes two of the most volatile issues in America, mixes them, and throws it against the wall."

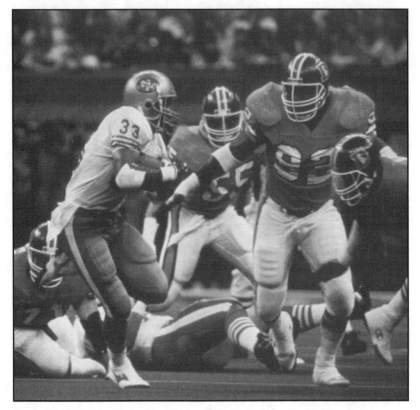

Roger Craig ran for 69 yards and a touchdown and caught five passes from Montana for another 34 yards. (Photo©Vernon Biever)

Tagliabue told us that Dr. Tenant's lab did not conduct the testing for the NFL during the '89 season. But the TV story, he said, omitted that information.

"You would think," the new commissioner said, "that Dr. Tenant were under the podium here testing me."

Clean hands? The NFL would continue to be in good hands. Paul Tagliabue showed to be smooth and slick as Pete Rozelle's successor. The NFL had its continuity, too.

Sure did. Paul Tagliabue's first Super Bowl party down at the Convention Center near the Mississippi River was the same kind of thing that Pete Rozelle had tossed. Folks begged for invitations, offered high prices for them. The party theme was LaFete, like out of Mardi Gras.

Powder-wigged performers made out to be plantation aristo-crats danced to a flute and string sextet inside the front door. It was the Old South, recreated. Then were the long lines, the taste of gumbo, sushi, oysters, clams and mussels. As usual, I got out of there early, in a bad mood.

Jazz combos played in the middle of the streets of the French Quarter on Saturday afternoon. Mobs of visitors in 49ers red and Broncos orange paraded along Bourbon Street in the sunshine, gripping the customary plastic cups filled with booze. Football seemed to be America's excuse to get drunk.

I went to the wharf and took a paddle-wheel ferry across the Mississippi. Then I drove out to Dick Schaap's party along a bayou, where it was quiet, and pigged out on ribs and jambolaya. It seems there's always an old place-kicker at Dick's party, and this one was no exception. Jan Stenerud was there, and he relived Super Bowl IV for me, especially the three field goals he kicked to send the Chiefs ahead of the Vikings, 9-0.

That had been the Other League's last game, and the Chiefs had played with AFL-10 patches on their shoulders. Through the '70s, the AFC's successor had dominated this Super Bowl. Now the NFC, with its roots to the old NFL, dominated again. NFC clubs had won five Super Bowls in succession, seven of eight. It was an imbalance to concern the new commissioner.

◆   ◆   ◆

On the footbridge outside the Superdome, memorabilia col-lectors eyed our Super Bowl XXIV press badges. They were offer-ing $100 for a pin.

Someplace, scattered at home, I have them all, 24 of them, the little medallions they gave us at Super Bowls I and II, and the pins, I thought. I wonder what the whole set would be worth?

Nope. Just a flash thought. Priceless. They symbolized so many good memories to me.

◆   ◆   ◆

San Francisco quarterback Joe Montana looks for another receiver in the 49ers' 55-10 rout of the Broncos in Super Bowl XXIV. Montana, who completed 22 passes for five touchdowns, was named the game's MVP, the third time he has won the honor. (Photo©Vernon Biever)

This year there were no bolting horses. No booming cannons. No recreation of the Battle of New Orleans. No New Orleans stripper prancing topless along the sidelines. All these memories of Super Bowls past flashed by.

Instead, there were just the usual twinges of patriotism. A copy of the Statue of Liberty was wheeled in, and an enormous American flag descended from the roof. The crowd gave a standing ovation for the Panama invaders. Then Aaron Neville lip-synced *The Star-Spangled Banner.*

Denver won the toss, as the London bookies watched in the middle of the night in England.

And then John Elway took the first snap from the Denver 23. He passed and threw wild low, yards from his receiver, Mark Jackson. Oooops. An omen, I thought. Then Elway tried a pass on second down. Wild low a second time. Denver had to punt.

Joe Montana missed his first pass, too. Then Roger Craig ran around the left end for 18 yards. You could see the angry talking on the field. The Broncos seemed to want to fight. Montana guided the 49ers down to the Broncos' 20. Then he looked right — no receiver open — left, no receiver — then over the middle. Jerry Rice was drifting free, and Montana hit him. Rice broke off the Broncos' shoddy tackle attempts at a touchdown.

Elway managed to bring the Broncos back to the 49ers' 25. Then he missed three passes. David Treadwell, the Broncos' new kicker, booted a 42-yard field goal. It was San Francisco 7-3 midway through the first quarter.

Next, the Broncos stopped the 49ers. They had the ball at their 49, starting with decent field position. Bobby Humphrey fumbled the ball away on the first play.

Joe Montana had the ball again and passed to Rice for 20 yards. A few plays later he passed to Rice for 21. The 49ers moved to the 7. Montana passed to Brent Jones, the tight end, for the touchdown. Mike Cofer missed the point after. San Francisco was up, 13-3, when the first quarter ended.

Elway threw some more incompletions as the second quarter began. Denver punted again. Montana had the ball again and passed to Tom Rathman for 18 and then 12. Craig ripped off some runs. At the 1, Montana handed off to Rathman, who bashed in. San Francisco was up, 20-3.

With 1:38 left before the halftime show, Montana had another chance. He worked the 49ers from their 41 to the Broncos' 38. Forty seconds showed on the clock. On second-and-one, Joe went the distance and hit Rice for the 38-yard touchdown. It was San Francisco 27-3 at the half. Elway had gone six-for-20.

The halftime show featured Snoopy on his 40th birthday.

On his first pass of the second half, Elway missed his receiver again. Michael Walter intercepted. Montana, on the first play, hit Rice again for the touchdown, 28 yards. It was Rice's third TD. San Francisco was up, 34-3.

On Denver's next series, Chet Brooks intercepted Elway. Brooks ran the ball back 38 yards. Montana threw this time to John Taylor, for 35 yards, for his fifth touchdown pass. San Francisco was up, 41-3. And we were just a bit into the third quarter.

But . . . but . . . John Elway took the Broncos on a drive now. They went 61 yards, with Humphrey running 34 in one burst. Elway scored the TD himself, running in from the 3. The Broncos had cut the 49ers' lead to 41-10.

On the 49ers' next series, Montana completed four of five passes. Rathman scored the touchdown from the 3 on the first play of the fourth quarter. San Francisco was up, 48-10.

On the field, Matt Millen, the refugee from the Raiders, stuck his tongue out at Elway. Elway barked back.

Millen said something. Joking later, he said he'd said: "`Now that I'm in San Francisco, I'm a closet homosexual and I can come out.' He laughed. No, I told him to keep his spirits up."

The 49ers chased Elway as he tried to flee their pass rush. He was hit behind the line and fumbled. Daniel Stubbs picked it up for the Niners and rumbled 15 yards to the 1. Roger Craig scored on the next play. San Francisco was up, 55-10.

Montana left the game to a standing ovation. When the Broncos got the ball again, Elway was out of the game, too.

Elway knelt near the bench and rested his hand on his helmet. A memory flashed back of the thrice-beaten Francis Tarkenton years before sitting on his helmet at another Super Bowl.

The final was San Francisco 55, Denver 10. That made it six straight Super Bowls for the NFC. San Francisco 4-0, and Denver 0-4.

America bemoaned another lopsided Super Bowl. I thought back to what I had written years before, before Pete Rozelle's first

Super Bowl. The game was another resounding dud. But the 49ers, they were the colossus.

The greatest quarterback ever, they said to Joe Montana.

"As I've been saying," Montana said, rejecting the notion, "those things are reserved for the guys who are no longer in the game."

The next morning, George Seifert, with his gray hair and wire-rimmed eyeglasses familiar to all of TV-America, was hailed as a hero, as he conducted the winning coach's press conference. When it was over, he went to rejoin his team to fly back to San Francisco and the victory parade on Market Street.

But now he was standing outside the Hyatt, alone, a forlorn figure in the New Orleans gloom, hands in pockets, unnoticed, looking lost, waiting for his ride.

"We Come to Win...Period"

Shannon Sharpe was noted for his loquacious logic before he ever reached the stage at the Super Bowl.

For example, Sharpe, the Broncos' tight end, arrived in San Diego having already spoken the following:

"You're only great if you win. I mean, Alexander wasn't Alexander the Mediocre or Alexander the Average. He was Alexander the Great, and there's a reason for it."

That makes sense.

And . . .

After Mike Holmgren fessed up that the Packers had allowed the Broncos to score in the final two minutes of Super Bowl XXXII to give Bret Favre more time to mount a counterattack, Sharpe was hit upon by an ESPN reporter in Hawaii at the Pro Bowl. The question implied that the Broncos' victory, somehow, was tainted. A bit dirty. Not clean.

"'We let them score,'" Sharpe said in his best Green Bay taunting, mimicking voice.

"Did they let us score the other 24 points, too?"

That makes sense.

And there were the daily quotes and comments that endeared Sharpe to the media during the prelude to the Super Bowl.

The daily scene went pretty much like this: It was Mike Shanahan's required function to deliver the daily wake-up call (hah) to the energetic journalists in the meeting room at the La Jolla Hyatt. These ink-stained wretches and other modern media marvels had awakened at 6:30 in the morning at the San Diego Marriott to catch the NFL's 7:15 bus. Shanahan's pearls would be doled out at 8:30, sharp. Out of generosity, or pity, the NFL had arranged for Danish pastries, bagels and muffins to be stacked on trays; hot coffee and orange juice to be available from cisterns — no Bloody Marys — so that the cream of American journalism did not have to listen to Shanahan on empty stomachs.

After Shanahan had droned through his monologue about practice and his feelings for John Elway and Terrell Davis, he answered several questions.

Then the Broncos players straggled in to sit either at podiums or round tables with white table clothes.

Shannon Sharpe became the counterpoint to his own head coach. He had trained for these pre-Super Bowl moments for years. With the same solitude that a football coach watches game films in the midnight dark, Sharpe stood in front of a mirror and talked to it.

"Every night I would stand for 20 minutes in the mirror, talking to myself," Sharpe told the media. "I'd be the reporter and interviewee.

"Sometimes I'd stumble and mumble, but I got to where I could speak fluently. I could just flow and not get twisted up in the words and not babble on, but be concise and candid."

So, Shannon, what about playing the Packers Sunday? A gaggle of reporters were around him. Unlike standing before the mirror, he did not have to go both ways. Just be the interviewee. He had his rapturous audience, as once upon a time Joe Namath did at Super Bowl III when he guaranteed the Jets would win.

"I'm not Joe Namath," Sharpe assured the journalists. "I can't guarantee it for the simple fact that I don't touch the ball every time.

"If I touched the ball every time, I'd guarantee the win."

He did promise that he'd humble the Packers' defensive backs.

"If they cover me one-on-one and beat my butt, I'll renounce my citizenship, leave the country and leave all my assets in a bank account in your name," he said.

A couple of Denver columnists started planning trips to Hawaii.

"We come to win this game," Sharpe told them. "Period. Anything less than a win for the Denver Broncos is unacceptable.

"Not John passing for 400 yards and we lose. Not Terrell rushing for 200 yards and we lose. We don't come here to play well for the AFC.

"We come to win this game. Period."

This was the finest material of the entire Super Bowl week.

The Broncos were simmering about the aura of invincibility we the media placed around Favre and the Packers. The Denver team was regarded as cannon fodder. It was a game. That meant two teams. The Packers had to have somebody to beat.

"What got me all riled up," Sharpe told the press after his virtual guarantee, "they make us seem like we're a high school team in Green Bay.

"But we're all professional athletes. There's a reason why we're here."

Braggadocio at the Super Bowl is quite common. It dates back to Fred Williamson, The Hammer, at Super Bowl I. He got himself hammered by the Packers. Hollywood Henderson got himself ridiculed.

Clairvoyance, on the other hand, is rare. Football coaches, if they could, would stick old socks into the mouths of their athletes to keep them from saying anything that might inflame the opposition. But Namath did deliver.

So would Sharpe.

Throughout the Super Bowl week, there was a subplot.

On Tuesday morning, among the Media Day mob, there was a smiling, familiar-looking figure. His name was Sterling Sharpe and just a few years earlier he had been a premier pass receiver, perhaps the equal of Jerry Rice.

Sterling Sharpe played — for the Green Bay Packers, when they were a team in development. In 1994, he dislodged two cervical vertebrae in his neck. The doctors told Sterling Sharpe never to play football again.

Sterling is Shannon's big brother. They grew up on a farm in Georgia, learned to play football. Sterling went to South Carolina. Shannon to Savannah State.

When he played in Green Bay, Sterling Sharpe had a rule. He would not talk to the media. He was mum, the total opposite of his kid brother who had joined the Denver Broncos as a seventh-round draft choice. No answers from Sterling, no hellos, no goodbyes. No explanation.

Funny, he did not have a sock in his mouth. When he was forced to leave football part way through what could have been a Hall of Fame career, he became a football analyst for ESPN.

There are times, on set, when Sterling Sharpe can even outtalk Joe Theismann.

Now this ESPN-paid member of the media first tried to dodge the rest of the media. At last he stopped briefly to proclaim his allegiance in the Super Bowl.

". . . my brother is my brother," said Sterling Sharpe in rare public words issued when not on his own ESPN set. "Before I had Green Bay in the NFL, or any catches, or any touchdowns, I had Shannon Sharpe as a brother."

"I play for my brother," Shannon told the media. "He basically plays the game through me."

Nobody on the Packers was able to beat Shannon Sharpe's butt in Super Bowl XXXII. In this game, he caught five passes from Elway. He blocked strongly for Davis.

"I think they bought into a situation where they were heavy favorites, with Favre the three-time MVP," Sharpe said in the postgame interview tent. "It doesn't matter. They have an excellent football team.

"Any other AFC team, they would have folded, but not a Mike Shanahan-coached team."

Three days earlier, Sharpe said the Broncos had come to win the game and they did. Only he had had the audacity to come out and say they would to a flock of journalists.

It was Shannon Sharpe who went to Hawaii, his bank account enlarged and still in his own name.

Super Bowl Ticket Prices

Game	Price(s)	Game	Price(s)
I	$12, $10, $6	XVII	$40
II	$12	XVIII	$60
III	$12	XIX	$60
IV	$15	XX	$75
V	$15	XXI	$75
VI	$15	XXII	$100
VII	$15	XXIII	$100
VIII	$15	XXIV	$125
IX	$20	XXV	$150
X	$20	XXVI	$150
XI	$20	XXVII	$175
XII	$30	XXVIII	$175
XIII	$30	XXIX	$200
XIV	$30	XXX	$350, $250, $200
XV	$40	XXXI	$275
XVI	$40	XXXII	$275

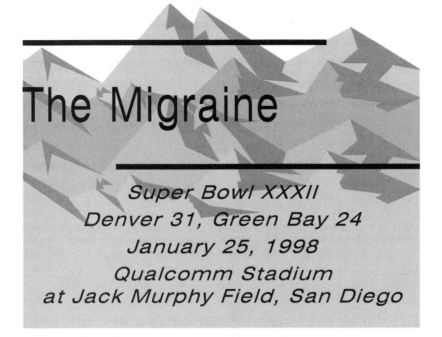

The Migraine

Super Bowl XXXII
Denver 31, Green Bay 24
January 25, 1998
Qualcomm Stadium
at Jack Murphy Field, San Diego

We straggled out of the Marriott Hotel at the Marina in San Diego, a motley crew. We were off to see the Broncos and John Elway, Terrell Davis, Bill Romanowski, Mike Shanahan; the Packers and Bret Favre, Reggie White, Dorsey Levens, Mike Holmgren.

"Busses, where are the busses?"

It was the traditional Super Bowl question, asked by a wailing waif, lost in the crowd.

From the time of Joe Namath on, the NFL's propaganda specialists had spirited us out to the annual Media Day aboard chartered busses. It was the annual Super Bowl ride.

No busses this time.

They had us cross the street and there, lined up, were bright red San Diego trolleys waiting for the mob of journalists. We were prepared to pepper new brilliant questions at the men who would play or coach in a Sunday football game. Even Bill Clinton would take time out from whatever he was doing at the White House to watch on television.

They had us line up, a herd of sheeplike zombies, to get aboard the cars. Guys came crashing across the street from the hotel, jayrunning. I wound up in the last seat on the last car, across from a chap from a London paper.

The trolley started. It was not the sort of trolley that had ridden the streets of America's cities in the 1930s — powered by electric lines overhead. What once upon a time was called a streetcar. The San Diego trolley was really a red train, a modern version of public transportation.

Only a southern California imagination would call this very efficient mode of travel a trolley.

It purred along through San Diego, hooked a right turn. Mountains could be seen in the distance. And all along, the writing rabble talked, talked, talked.

Twenty minutes later the red train arrived at the new stop for Qualcomm Stadium at Jack Murphy Field. With multimillion dollar payouts to players, a salary cap and a $17.6 billion TV contract, the names of America's playing fields were now for sale.

Ten years earlier when the Redskins beat the Broncos at Super Bowl XXII with a 15-minute assault, San Diego's stadium had been named Jack Murphy. It was the only stadium in the world named after a journalist. Jack Murphy had been sports columnist of the *San Diego Union* for years. He had campaigned first for a pro team, then a place for that team to play.

He was honored by having the stadium named for him. We, his journalist friends, were honored by association. But then San Diego had trouble funding renovations for its stadium for its second Super Bowl, scheduled for 1998. The Qualcomm people rushed into the breech waving green stuff. For $20 million, San Diego renamed the stadium for a corporation and as a sop to the town's citizens, tagged Jack Murphy's name at the end.

Now we were there clogged into a runway on a dank, dreary Tuesday morning. They kept us there, shoving, gossiping, until the Broncos in their new blue uniforms marched out onto the field below. The stars of the team were led to special podiums to accommodate the packs of journalists wishing to hear their wise words.

◆   ◆   ◆

With the knowledge that anyone with a Luger pistol, or the instinct to trade souvenirs, could obtain an official Paul Tagliabue-sanctioned Super Bowl XXXII pin, the NFL had come up with the idea of photo IDs. Such a laminated ID card dangling around our necks on color coded lanyards would grant us entrance into all media functions. The Media Day festivities. The various press conferences. The media headquarters in the San Diego Convention Center next to the Marriott. The media hospitality room, where every afternoon at tea time, local food emporiums would offer a freeload. Best of all was Bill Egner's APS pizza popping machine that turned out small, tasty circular pizza pies at an assembly line rate.

The only lines longer all week than at the pizza machine were at the NFL's ID cameras. A serendipitous line crossed the media credential hallway. I jumped at the end. In exactly 57 minutes, 48 point 38 seconds I was in the front of the line and about to get my picture taken. Always on the alert to check out the NFL's efficiency, I had snapped on my stopwatch.

By the time I was issued by photo card with the red — coded for print medium — lanyard, an entire hour had been spent without yet qualifying to stand on the pizza line.

Soon after pizza we headed for the Gaslamp District, San Diego's quaint, artistic area for tourists. Not quite Bourbon Street, but it wasn't Pontiac, Michigan, either.

◆   ◆   ◆

Once the NFL security specialists had funneled the 3,000 sheep/journalists down the one open ramp to the field at Qualcomm Stadium, I parked myself near Terrell Davis.

Davis had grown up in San Diego, played for George Allen at Long Beach State and then for Georgia. He had run for 1,750 yards during the season, the champion runner of the AFC. Superb figures, if not quite the 2,053 Barry Sanders had gained with his spectaculars for the Lions — who had not won a championship since 1957, a decade before the first Super Bowl.

Davis stood in the row of podiums, just beyond John Elway at Podium No. 1 and Mike Shanahan, the coach, at Podium No. 2. Up on the scoreboard, the game clock counted down second by second from one hour to the end of the session, when we'd be funneled back off the turf through the single open gate.

Somebody in the semicircle hit Davis with a question about the might of the Packers — with 345-pound (at least) Gilbert Brown in the middle and Reggie White on the same defensive line.

"To be the best you have to beat the best," Davis said.

Then he was asked if he was scared.

"Spiders scare me off the field," said Davis. "Rats scare me. Critters. Anything."

Not Packers.

"I sit in my room and can't believe I'm here," said Davis. "Which is probably good. I'm keeping my cool."

> *"I sit in my room and can't believe I'm here. Which is probably good. I'm keeping my cool."*
> *— Terrell Davis*

Davis' words were halted abruptly by the squealing ring of a cellular telephone. Any of us who exist in the '90s would never dream of attending a Super Bowl Media Day without our mobile phones. The state-of-the-art status symbol. Never know when the guy 10 yards away might want to call about dinner plans.

I made an end run around a phone talker — and was struck to a halt by one of the media marvels. She was adorned in a skirt that dipped to her high thighs which were covered by net stockings — and her spiked heels dug into the soft earth of the football sideline area. The clip on her microphone proclaimed that she was reporting for *The Daily Show*.

She was identified by other curious reporters as Beth Littleford. And Beth asked a blushing Bronco to lift her into the air. He managed to hoist her above his head five times, establishing a Super Bowl record for the human push and jerk. The record would later be bested by the Packers' John Michels, all of this recorded by San Diego's TV station KFMB.

Meanwhile, some dude walked through the media mob wearing a cowboy hat and a football uniform. His jersey was half Broncos and half Packers. The name panel on back identified him as Faway. This Favre/Elway creature wore Dallas Cowboys pants. Somebody identified him as the cowboy character from *The Keenan Ivory Wayans Show*. I'm just guessing, but I figure it is show that I must catch some day on TV.

It was time for Super Bowl XXXII Media Day Breakfast II. Before we got to meet the Packers up close and so on.

◆   ◆   ◆

It was at Super Bowl XX that a helicopter buzzed over the Bears' practice field in New Orleans. A TV camera poked out of the chopper. The Bears were observed . . . oh, lined up with five linemen, two wideouts, a tight end, a quarterback and two running backs, one of them Walter Payton. William (The Refrigerator) Perry cast a shadow over the offense.

It is NFL policy, when its forbidden air space is invaded by spies, peeking media, groupies or aliens from the planet Jupiter, to sound a warning, then light up the missile launcher. In the Bears' case, Jim McMahon provided the counter attack by mooning the helicopter. It drifted away.

Now the Broncos were similarly threatened at practice for the Super Bowl. They drilled at the Chargers' practice field, an expanse located in a place named Murphy Canyon.

The chopper pulled off traffic-reporting duties by San Diego station KFMB-TV, a CBS outlet, churned above.

John Elway opted against dropping his drawers to thwart the intruder. Rather, Mike Shanahan went apoplectic. Well, not quite.

"It was inappropriate," Shanahan told Denver writers later.

He discussed the situation with the station bosses and was informed that KFMB was doing a piece on Super Bowl security.

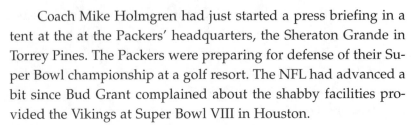

Coach Mike Holmgren had just started a press briefing in a tent at the at the Packers' headquarters, the Sheraton Grande in Torrey Pines. The Packers were preparing for defense of their Super Bowl championship at a golf resort. The NFL had advanced a bit since Bud Grant complained about the shabby facilities provided the Vikings at Super Bowl VIII in Houston.

Holmgren was deep into parrying a question about a traditional Super Bowl week rumor — that he would become general manager of the Seattle Seahawks. "Premature," he said.

Just then a jet crossed over the tent drowning out further bits of wisdom. When the noise let up, Holmgren said:

"First helicopters. Now jets. Nothing's sacred around here."

This is a man who had already gained Lombardian stature in Green Bay. It was years before Green Bay named a street in honor of Lombardi. The Green Bay suburb of Ashwaubenon named a street Holmgren Way after just one championship, obviously a symbol of the fast-to-react '90s.

And for sure, Super Bowl XXXII was important stuff on the Internet. Excerpts from a column by Jerry Green on www.cbsportsline.com:

———————————

SAN DIEGO — Vince Lombardi once said of himself:

"This is a game for madmen. In football, we're all mad. I've been called a tyrant. But I've also been called the coach with the simplest system in football, and I suppose there is some truth to both of those.

"The perfect name for the perfect coach would be Simple Simon Legree."

The Migraine

The voice was gruff, gravel, often spitting anger. It was a New York voice, transplanted to the warm heart of America's Midwest.

To those who knew him when the Green Bay Packers were the precisioned conquerors of the 1960s, that voice grates the memory even now. He was a dictator, a man of discipline and intimidation, and a perfectionist.

These images remain 28 years after his death. There is Lombardi on the sidelines, in the Fedora and camel's hair overcoat, his breath vaporizing in the crisp Green Bay air, the gap between his front teeth.

Flash ahead, three decades.

Mike Holmgren said of himself:

"Trying to live up to Vince Lombardi and what went on there for that stretch, it's almost an impossible task . . .

"I'm proud of how we built this thing up, I really am."

The voice is mellow, soft, no trace of anger. If it carries a trace of an accent, it is a West Coast voice. He most often shuns hats and he wears a Packers green jacket or shirt on the sidelines. His mustache is bristly.

Again the Packers are the precisioned conquerors, now in the 1990s. If the Packers beat the Broncos Sunday in Super Bowl XXXII, Holmgren would match Lombardi's achievements in this event that now captivates America.

It didn't back then, back when Lombardi took his haughty champion Packers to Los Angeles to play the Kansas City Chiefs in what history would record as Super Bowl I.

The then-and-now, as Holmgren refers to the two Super Bowl eras in Green Bay, can be capsuled in the styles of the two football coaches . . .

Lombardi's Packers won five NFL championships in seven years. They won the first two Super Bowls, when the NFL establishment felt contempt for the upstart American Football League. The leagues had settled their war and merged in 1966. The result was the Super Bowl. In the first Super Bowl, the Packers dissected the Chiefs, 35-10. In victory for himself and his league, Lombardi tried diplomacy . . .

Vince Lombardi never could have tolerated standing on a podium with furry microphones over his head, a mob shoving to get closer.

At this Super Bowl XXXII, Holmgren told the story of how he stopped in the lobby of the Packers' offices when he went to Green Bay for his job interview. He gawked at the collage of photographs of Lombardi and his Packers and of two Super Bowl trophies.

"When the next coach comes walking in that lobby," Holmgren said, "maybe our team of the last two years, we'll have some pictures up there, too.

"And they can get a sense of then-and-now."

Fans — Super Bowl fans represent much of the American mentality of the late 20th century. We are a party nation. Inhibited behavior is not the fashion of the era.

Rather, the fashion plates from Wisconsin flew in in their charters, or drove their RVs two-thirds across the breadth of the continent to get to San Diego. Once in California, the Green Bay fans were met by the fashion plate for Denver.

This would be a game of styles.

The Cheeseheads vs. the Barrelman.

Green Bay is more than merely the toilet paper citadel of America. It is more than the small town with a major-league football franchise owned publicly by the citizens. It is located in a state famous for its cheese — and thus thousands of Green Bay fans roamed San Diego's Gaslamp District with yellow foam-rubber wedges on their heads.

These were the Cheeseheads, the most devoted of Packers fans. They were rabid, they were faithful — these folks from the heartland of Middle America. They were basically conservative people with two weaknesses, their passion for the Packers, and a failure to realize how absurd they looked with a large hunk of fake cheese lousing up their hairdos.

But then, they were better dressed than Denver's Barrelman.

The Barrelman strolled around town adorned in a flame orange cowboy hat, flame orange cowboys boots and a flame orange metal drum, or barrel, held over his bare torso by blue suspenders.

The Migraine

When the Broncos' Super Bowl XXXII charter landed at San Diego's Lindbergh Field, the Barrelman was on the tarmac. He stood at attention, his flame-orange right glove in salute. The same military salute Terrell Davis flashed to his teammates when he scored a touchdown.

The Barrelman's name is Tim McKernan. And it is unknown what he wears under his barrel, if anything, or if he has ever lifted up *Daily Show* reporter Beth Littleford.

Norm Clarke of Denver's *Rocky Mountain News* encountered the Barrelman at Media Day and reported this conversation:

"Do you prefer boxers or briefs?"

Barrelman: "I can honestly say neither."

"Thong maybe?"

Barrelman : "No comment."

Reveling in the publicity, McKernan was wearing his barrel at his fifth Super Bowl. He has never lost his barrel. Actually, he told reporters looking for color that he started his barrel-wearing when he discovered a discarded steel drum at the United Airlines hangar in Denver, where he worked as a mechanic. He made a $10 bet that he would wear it to a game. He did — Monday Night Football.

Since then he said, he'd worn out 15 barrels. Once he was offered $500 to drop the barrel and answer one of the most pressing questions in the history of pro football.

He declined. "I told them I could never afford the fine," he said.

◆   ◆   ◆

It's a good thing the Barrelman was along to provide a touch of color.

Mike Shanahan's press briefings were battleship gray.

An example or two:

"I thought practice went well yesterday. We had special teams practice for about forty minutes and our normal practice lasted about an hour and twenty minutes., about ten or fifteen minutes less than we normally practice on Wednesday."

"We'd like to be able to run the football like we have all year. I think that's going to be a key, to keep that offensive team off the field. Favre, when he's on the field, he's got the opportunity to make big plays."

Meat and potatoes stuff.

Shanahan was regarded among the 1980s group of young potential-genius assistant coaches who topped the gossip lists of the head-coach rumor quacks at prior Super Bowls. He was an assistant coach under Dan Reeves for the Broncos, then got his chance as a head coach when Al Davis hired him to coach the Los Angeles Raiders in 1988.

Coaching the Raiders is a perilous situation for an ambitious coach. Shanahan survived a season and a quarter under Davis. Fired in midseason, he rejoined the Broncos as an assistant before the bullet holes healed. He moved on and became offensive coordinator for the 49ers. Coaching is a merry-go-round occupation. The man Shanahan succeeded with the 49ers was Mike Holmgren, who advanced to become head coach of the Packers.

Unlike most of those young potential geniuses who become head coaches and are soon overmatched, Shanahan did get a second chance, as QB coach for Elway. The Broncos made it to their fourth Super Bowl that season — the 55-10 loss to the 49ers. In '92, the 49ers summoned him to become George Seifert's offensive coordinator. Now he could work with Steve Young. With the 49ers, Shanahan would appear in his fourth Super Bowl — and first victory — as Young broke Joe Montana's records at Super Bowl XXIX.

After three seasons in San Francisco, Shanahan was recalled to Denver for his third tour with the Broncos. This time he would be head coach, succeeding Wade Phillips, who had succeeded Reeves two years earlier.

Now he had Elway — his strong supporter — and a team in the Super Bowl. But now he had to sit for the grilling as a head coach for the first time. And in front of him was the probing press at the Broncos' encampment at the Hyatt Regency La Jolla.

"I never did talk to Mike after I took his place," he said in response to a query about the Holmgren-Shanahan linkage. "Once you leave an organization, I think the feeling is, 'He's gone, he's doing his thing. Now we've got to keep our organization intact and focus from within.'"

Shanahan wasn't there to thrill the media.

Focus was Mike Shanahan's word from the coaches' code book. But it is duly reported that the earth does not stop its spin on Super Bowl week, although we the media also have focus. Of sorts.

Out of Washington came new reports that football fan Bill Clinton was trapped in another sex scandal — true or not, powerful enough to blast the Super Bowl off front pages across America except in Green Bay.

Pope John selected this very week to visit the infidel Fidel Castro in Cuba.

So it was that one ink-stained wretch tested Shanahan on the power of his focus.

"To be honest, I have been aware of it," Shanahan said of the news involving the prez and Pope. "Any time you have CNN in your room, going through some of the channels, I was able to see a few of those things with the president and the Pope.

"I guess I'm supposed to say that I'm isolated and don't know any of that, but I do read a little bit."

It is impossible for the most dedicated of reporters — an oxymoron? — to catch every word spoken, or even to read every press release pumped out by the NFL's and other hanger-on propagandists.

I missed one myself.

A press release:

"Super Bowl As Science?

"San Diego State University Presents

"Pre-Super Bowl Scientific Congress . . .

"TOPICS INCLUDE . . .

"Newspaper Critics Look at Super Bowl Television

"Media Leaders Speak Out on Marv Albert Trial . . . "

Shucks, I was in the wrong place again. Just when the media leaders were reenacting the Marv Albert Trial, perhaps even with teethmarks, I had been at Qualcomm Stadium on the morning of Media Day.

Too late as always.

◆　　◆　　◆

But I did encounter my longtime friend Woody Paige, sports columnist for the *Denver Post* and one of the rare innovative guys in our profession.

"Did you know Terrell Davis killed George Allen?" said Woody.

I professed total ignorance. I knew Allen, the Flimflam Man who coached the Redskins at Super Bowl VII, had finished his career coaching a college team at Long Beach State. He died soon after a football season.

"Davis was at Long Beach State," said Paige. "They won their last game. They doused George Allen with Gatorade. George Allen got pneumonia and died. Davis was one of those who doused Allen with the Gatorade."

Great story. Davis claimed innocence. He maintained that he did not have his hand on the Gatorade barrel.

◆　　◆　　◆

The media headquarters was stacked with out-of-town newspapers. Free for the journalists to scrutinize. Denver, Green Bay, Milwaukee, Los Angeles.

"Hell, I wish I had that thing in the Green Bay paper," said my friend Dallas.

"You mean the ad in the sports section."

My friend Newark snickered. We were Super Bowl veterans, campaign ribbons across the fronts of our sweat suits.

The *Green Bay Press-Gazette* had been had. Among all the idolatry articles about the Packers in the front section where most newspapers place news, the *Press-Gazette* ran a half-page advertisement from Denver's radio station KBPI. It said essentially:

"Future world champs rock the Cheeseheads & carve Brett Favre . . . Packers fans call us & admit you're losers !!"

What the ad essentially said if you happened to fold the page in a certain way:

"Bleep the Packers."

More responsible journalism was featured in the *Milwaukee Journal Sentinel*, which dispatched an intrepid columnist to the California beaches to track the Pack at play. One Kathy Flanagan, penning a sports pages column entitled *The Ocean Effect*, claimed to have traced Brett Favre to the Belly Up Bar in Solana Beach, near La Jolla.

She informed her panting readers:

" . . . *it didn't take a detective to see football's three-time MVP shaking his talented bottom on stage with a young woman on each side of him . . . etc.*"

Heavens to Joe Willie Namath in Fort Lauderdale and John Matuszak on Bourbon Street.

◆　　◆　　◆

As the week wore on, one of the more pressing questions was would Bill Romanowski provide an encore for the TV millions around the globe.

Journalists had surrounded Romanowski every morning when access was available to press him on his game plan.

Romanowski played linebacker for the Broncos with an attitude. During the exhibition season, against the Carolina Panthers, he busted quarterback Kerry Collins' jaw with a hit. The league fined him 20 grand.

Then on Monday Night Football, Romanowski juiced up ABC's show by spitting into the face of the 49ers' J.J. Stokes. Instant replay had been removed from the NFL game. But ABC and then the sports shows on cable played the incident over and then some more, as TV is wont to do when it has nothing new.

The cause celebre was turned into a racial incident. Romanowski was called upon by coach Shanahan to meet with his teammates and explain his actions. He apologized. His teammates said they understood.

At the Super Bowl, the story flared again.

"If it hadn't been on television," Romanowski told the journalists — over and then some more, "well, it was on television. You could say it's happened before in the NFL. It's unacceptable. It showed no class."

Romanowski had already been a demon contributor on two Super Bowl championship teams in San Francisco.

Now seeking a third diamond ring, he told the eager journalists:

"I was geared up to play my old team. When emotions were high, logic was low. It was just not a smart move."

◆　　　◆　　　◆

This time no media busses took the gringo journalists to Tijuana to treat us with the world's largest Caesar Salad at Agua Caliente Racetrack.

It was a memory from 10 years past — the bus across the border into Mexico, greetings from the POLICIA and mayor. A police escort, Fiesta de Super Bowl. None of this. Instead Tijuana went to lure true tourists from Wisconsin and Colorado, hunting for bric-a-brac, with greenbacks stuffed in their jeans. Enough of the moochers from the media.

The Migraine

Rather, San Diego's Sea World opened its gates for a feed and show at what was billed as a Media Party.

We sat there in the cold and watched Shamu and its fellow whales perform all sorts of tricky aquatic aerobics while we risked getting splashed in the seats near the drink.

Actually, it was a neat show. It geared some of us up to visit with Gilbert Brown at the Packers' interview sessions in the morning.

◆   ◆   ◆

One of the quickest, safest get-rich-quick schemes for pro sports franchise owners is expansion. The plutocrats who own the teams do not have to submit to the wiles and whims of the TV network moguls. They do not have to incur the wrath of the citizens by making them cough up thousands for the privilege of coughing up more dough to buy tickets.

They just soak other egomaniacal plutocrats a couple of hundred million bucks for the opportunity to field expansion teams.

The Jacksonville Jaguars and Carolina Panthers were admitted to the NFL in 1995. The existing franchise proprietors were paid so much they were forced into generosity. They made available more seasoned performers than in any previous expansion stickup. That plus free agency and the salary-cap gimmick, enabled the Panthers and Jaguars to become very mature pro teams by their second seasons.

In fact, Jacksonville and Carolina came within one last step of trying to beat each other at Super Bowl XXXI. The two expansion franchises reached their conference championship games in their second seasons of life. Unhappily for those of us with a cynical bent, the Packers and New England Patriots eliminated the giggles by knocking off the Panthers and Jaguars. Respectively.

It was the Broncos, who received the first anguish from this expansion into maturity. Under Shanahan and with Elway excelling, the Broncos had gone 13-and-3 in 1996. They had the spiffiest record in the AFC. Their 13 victories were matched only by the 13-3 Packers in the NFC. A Green Bay-Denver Super Bowl in New Orleans in January '97 was widely predicted by the pundits on ESPN and know-it-alls everywhere.

The Broncos had a playoff bye and home-field advantage throughout the AFC Super Bowl eliminations. They would be at Mile High Stadium, in the icy weather, before their adoring fans and the Barrelman, through the AFC championship game.

Alas, the second-season Jaguars were the Broncos' first playoff foe, January 4, 1997. Upsets happen. But very few of this caliber: Jacksonville 30, Denver 27.

Such was the load the Broncos carried into training camp in July 1997. They went to Mexico City for their first exhibition game vs. the Dolphins. Elway felt a pain shoot up his right arm. He headed for the Broncos' bench. He had torn a tendon in the biceps of his passing arm, said trainer Steve Antonopolus.

Next day and the days following, the papers carried notices of John Elway's professional football death. The stories, and the fears, were somewhat exaggerated.

"When he first came off the field and I looked at him," Shanahan told the media at the Super Bowl, "I could see a look in his eye that was different. He just pointed to his biceps, and there was some deformity there. And he gave me that look, 'Hey, this isn't good. I did something . . . '"

The trainer walked to Shanahan with the diagnosis.

"What does it mean?" Shanahan asked Antonopolus. "Can he play? Is that a season-ending injury?"

"No, I believe you can play without a biceps tendon," said Antonopolus to the fretting coach.

Shanahan continued with the story:

". . . to me, amazing, three or four days later he was throwing with less pain than before he got hurt.

"So it was a blessing in disguise."

Elway started the season. The Broncos won their first six games, nine of their first 10. They were dominating the AFC. Elway was having another vintage season. And Terrell Davis, the one-time sixth-round draft choice from Long Beach State and Georgia, had become the most productive running back in the AFC.

With the season headed toward another first-place finish, the Broncos took a pratfall. They were beaten in three of their last six games, including the spit-incident game at San Francisco. Stung, they whipped the Chargers in their last game and finished a game behind the Chiefs in the West, but at 12-and-4 still with the second-best record in the AFC.

They were in the playoffs as a wild card — one game at Mile High, then the rest of the games, if any, in hostile, foreign stadiums.

The first playoff game would be a rematch against Jacksonville. Year-old scars burned the Broncos.

It seems a Bronco never forgets. On December 27, 1997, it was Denver 42, Jacksonville 17. Elway and Davis were magnificent. John completed 16 of 24 passes. Davis rushed for 184 yards. The Broncos poured it on with three touchdowns in the fourth quarter.

Into the new year, it was on to Kansas City for the next playoff game. The Broncos and Chiefs had split their two regular-season games. In bitter, chilly weather, their playoff game became a suspenseful classic. Early in the fourth quarter, the Broncos were behind and it was third-and-five at the Chiefs' 44. Elway did what he always did best. He got distance on third down on a pass to Ed McCaffrey. Indeed, with McCaffrey's running after catching Elway's on-target strike, the play gained 43 yards to the one. Davis scored the touchdown — his second of the game — from there. It was the game winner. Denver 14, Kansas City 10.

It would be on to Pittsburgh for the AFC championship game.

In the 14th week of the schedule, the Broncos had gone into Pittsburgh. Davis was injured. The Steelers beat them, 35-24.

Now they played again before the wild Pittsburgh fans in Three Rivers Stadium. The Steelers went in front, 14-7. When it was 14-10, the Broncos defense treated Kordell Stewart, the young Steelers quarterback, to a lesson in playoff football. The defense got the ball back twice in the late moments before the intermission.

In the final 1:47 of the first half, Elway passed for two touchdowns. He went 15 yards to Howard Griffith and then one puny yard to McCaffrey with 13 seconds left in the half.

The Broncos were ahead — and their defense prevailed in the second half.

For the fifth time — the fourth time for Elway — the Broncos were in the Super Bowl. Denver 24, Pittsburgh 21.

◆   ◆   ◆

There is a basic reason some teams make it to Super Bowls — and others never do. That reason is smarts in the front office. Talent procurement.

In 1991, the Atlanta Falcons drafted Brett Favre as their quarterback of the future on the second round out of Southern Mississippi. They allowed him to play in two games all season. He threw five passes. He completed zero.

At this time, general manager Ron Wolf was endeavoring to rebuild the Packers' franchise from a quarter-century of futility in the post-Lombardi era. The franchise had won exactly one playoff game since winning Super Bowl II in 1968. Green Bay had lacked a qualified quarterback since Bart Starr.

On February 10, 1992, the Falcons offered Favre up in trade. Wolf grabbed him for the Packers in exchange for a first-round draft choice.

The rookie head coach welcomed Favre to the toilet paper town in Wisconsin.

"If Brett can stay healthy, he will be the cornerstone of our team for many years to come," the new coach said. The new coach's name was Mike Holmgren.

Smarts in the front office.

Favre patterned his style from another wild, untamed quarterback. He would run left and pass across his body to the right. He would throw from his knees. He was not a classic quarterback, but by his second season in Green Bay he was in the playoffs — and won a game.

The quarterback he emulated was named John Elway. Favre was nine years younger than Elway. They soon became friends.

Now Favre was at his second Super Bowl in January 1998. He had won his first. He was going for a second, his team heavily favored.

"To think of how many quarterbacks have played this game," Favre said, "and then think of a guy like John who has been to three, and now four, and has not won one. Jim Kelly. Dan Marino."

Elway. Marino. Kelly. They were in the fabled quarterback class of '83 — all drafted the same year. All would get to the Super Bowl. And lose. Elway was 0-for-3, Marino 0-for-1 and Kelly 0-for-4 in the Super Bowl.

> "To think of how many quarterbacks have played this game," Favre said, "and then think of a guy like John who has been to three, and now four, and has not won one."
>
> — Brett Favre

"It's amazing that I have an opportunity to do that in really just six years as a starter in this league," Favre said of his opportunity to become a two-time winner.

It was halfway through those six Green Bay seasons that Favre passed through a crisis.

Holmgren spoke about the relationship between coach and QB under the tent at the Packers' headquarters, uninterrupted by airplanes:

"Specifically, I think it happened about his fourth or fifth game his third year. His second year, you remember, we went to the playoffs and won a playoff game for the first time in a long time. He threw, I think twenty-five interceptions that year.

(Actually it was twenty-four.)

"In the off-season, he and I sat down. I feel the third year for a quarterback who has a chance to play, that should be the year where he let's you know exactly what type of player he's going to be. So he was entering his third year. My discussion with Brett, 'you got to eliminate the interceptions. There's a decision-making problem here and you should do this through a maturing process, an experience process.'

"I said 'if we have those games when things are going a little bit crazy I'm going to bring Mark (Brunell, then the backup) into the game and calm you down a little bit. We're not going to have a quarterback controversy.' That's what I said going into his third year . . .

"I didn't help him much by saying that. In the long run, maybe I did. At the time he was a little off-balanced. Then about the fifth game, I said, 'Look, you're the quarterback. You and I are joined at the hip.' It seemed to settle him down.

"More is made of our relationship than really is there.

"I said, 'We're either going to the top of the mountain together or we're going to wind up in the dumpster. But we'll be together.'"

And so they were, reigning Super Bowl champions as the 1997 season started.

As champions, the Packers did not get off to a glorious start. They were beaten in two of their first five games — by the Eagles, 10-9, when a field goal was missed, and by the Lions, when Favre had a relapse. The Lions picked him for three interceptions.

From then on, the Packers won 10 of their remaining 11 games. The lone loss was quite embarrassing. The Indianapolis Colts had not won in their first 10 games. Then they beat the champion, streaking Packers, 41-38, with a field goal with 0:00 on the clock.

That was a mere detour for Favre and Co.

They finished the season with a 13-3 record — same as the 49ers — and waltzed through the playoffs. First they upended the upstart Tampa Bay Buccaneers, 21-7, and in the NFC championship game they manhandled the 49ers and Steve Young in San

Francisco, 23-10. Favre was just OK in the two playoff games. But Dorsey Levens ran with brilliance. He gained 112 yards against the Bucs and 114 against the 49ers.

Las Vegas had no doubts about the Super Bowl. The Packers were immediately installed as 13-point favorites. And a lot of media sharpies figured it would be another Super Bowl rout — and the 14th victory in a row for the NFC.

At San Diego, a reporter asked Favre about the NFC's streak.

"Not only that streak and the NFC winning," he said, "you don't want to be the team Elway won on. Ten years, your kids, everybody will wonder 'what was the Super Bowl Elway won it?'

"Back in XXXII when I was playing. How embarrassing! I just want to make it very hard for him to get it."

On Friday morning, we were treated to the annual State of the NFL press conference by Commissioner Paul Tagliabue. Moments before the press conference, Tagliabue was escorted through the lobby of the San Diego Marriott by a half dozen security people and acolytes dressed in suits. It seemed the commissioner had his own Secret Service detail.

For sure, he attracted more media marvels for his press conference than Bill Clinton ever did at the White House.

He spoke to some thousand or so of us — and was as evasive, elusive as Barry Sanders on a 200-yard Sunday.

I remarked to my old Super Bowl friend, Lou Sahadi: "Tagliabue couldn't carry Pete Rozelle's jock."

But then Pete Rozelle never squeezed $17.6 billion from the TV networks to show America football games in the comfort of their own homes — or local pubs.

That night we all celebrated. It was the night of the annual Commissioner's Party. Several thousand of Tagliabue's closest friends and most severe critics. The theme was GO WEST — A State of Mind.

It was not a match for Rozelle's Cowboy party on the floor of the Astrodome, where you had to watch where you stepped, or the ranch party, or the one at Universal Studios, or the Airport at Miami, or the Naval Station last time in San Diego. But it was in a handy spot — the Convention Center not too many steps from the Marriott.

And not too many steps back, either.

◆   ◆   ◆

Super Bowl Sunday in San Diego started with a magnificent sunrise over the mountains to the east. The day was ideal — for football, for sailing, for fishing, for anything.

I caught an early bus out to Qualcomm Stadium at Jack Murphy Field. That was a good idea. No San Diego trolley this day. That was for the fans.

One thing constant about the Super Bowls through the years. It was a bussing event at Super Bowl I. It was a bussing event at Super Bowl XXXII.

Only there were more busses at SB XXXII.

So many that the committee folks had to import drivers from other cities. Ours was brought in from Las Vegas. He was given the exact NFL-sanctioned route to the stadium. He got lost trying to find his way out of downtown San Diego.

He finally found the way. And it was jammed the last two miles from Qualcomm.

Near the stadium and outside the gates, hustlers stood wall-to-wall engaged in the ticket trade. The scalpers were working between the stacked busses and cars, clogged in the traffic. The hottest Super Bowl ticket ever. They were going for $3,500 for two.

Once inside, I settled down in my seat. I was obviously in the gerontology row. My old friend Dick Schaap was to my left. Octogenarian Normie Miller was next to me on the right. Andy Rooney was a few seats away.

The NFL must have assigned the seats by age.

So what. We were there.

They introduced the players and coaches.

The Packers offense first. Favre was last. He ran through the Green Bay double files of players, arms raised. A photographer and his sound man went running through right behind Favre, capturing moving pictures for posterity of his posterior.

The Broncos, in their new home blue uniforms with the orange slashes, were then announced. The offense, also. Elway last. The same photographer and sound man ran behind him, grabbing closeup pictures of his uniform butt.

Last came Mike Shanahan. When he ran out, the Broncos' two files of players had dispersed. They were over by their bench, pounding each other over the shoulders, banging heads.

Shanahan ran out solo, untouched.

We proudly stood up for the traditional flyover of jets by the Navy's Blue Angels. Jewel, a local singer who was supposedly famous, sang *The Star-Spangled Banner*.

At last, a football game.

The Broncos kicked off and the Packers started from their 24. Favre escaped a sacking, made a key third-down play. And four minutes, two seconds into the Super Bowl, the Packers scored the first touchdown. Favre passed 22 yards to Antonio Freeman for the TD.

The Packers kicked off and the Broncos started from their 42. Elway made a key third-down pass. Davis broke for 27 yards to the Packers' 14. Elway ran for 10. Davis scored from the one and exchanged salutes with his teammates in the end zone.

It was 7-7. Each team had had the ball once and had marched long-distance for touchdowns. I thought back to those boring Super Bowls in which the coaches were scared to make mistakes. We were in for a weird, interesting game.

And about time.

The Broncos kicked off and the Packers, this time, started from their 27. But this time Favre was intercepted by Tyrone Braxton. at the Packers' 45.

Davis quickly ran around right end — Reggie White's side — for 16 yards. Seven plays and one Green Bay penalty later, the Broncos were at the one. Elway kept the ball and scored on the first play of the second period. The Broncos were ahead, 14-7.

The Broncos kicked off again and the Packers started from their 29. On the third play, Favre was flipped for a one-yard loss by Steve Atwater. Favre fumbled. Neil Smith recovered for the Broncos at the Packers' 33.

Now something truly mysterious was going on in the Broncos backfield. With the chance to go two touchdowns up, Terrell Davis was not on the field. He had rushed for 64 yards in the first quarter. Now Vaughn Hebron was in his tailback position. Davis was on the bench. The trainers were looking him over. He was twisting his neck. Bobbing his head.

Denver had to take a field goal this time — a 51-yarder by Jason Elam for a 17-7 lead.

The Broncos had had the ball three times and had scored three times on the mighty, heavily favored Packers.

Now the teams exchanged punts. Again Davis did not go out on offense. Derek Loville was in his spot. Elway failed to produce a first down. Denver's Tom Rouen punted the ball down on the Packers' five. A little more than 7½ minutes remained before the halftime spectacular.

The Broncos were in command — but what was keeping Terrell Davis out of the game?

On third down, Favre still stood at his own five, needing 10 yards. He hit Mark Chmura for 21 yards.

Bret Favre was still in the game.

Favre whittled through the Broncos defense the rest of the way — Levens running seven yards, passing to Robert Brooks for

Green Bay's Darius Holland tries to stop Denver running back Terrell Davis. Davis, rushed for 64 yards and a touchdown in the first quarter of Super Bowl XXXII before sitting out the second quater with a migraine headache. (Photo©James V. Biever)

three, Freeman for six and then nine, to Chmura for 11, Brooks again for 10.. With 17 seconds left, Favre looped the football toward the end zone from the six. Chmura leaped in the corner and hooked it down.

It was a magnificent march — and the Packers went into halftime down by the mere field goal, 17-14.

In the locker room, the Denver medics treated Terrell Davis — while outside we were treated to Motown Fortieth Anniversary music. The NFL, seizing on the old supply-and-demand economic theory, had sold sponsorship of the halftime show. It was the Royal Caribbean & Celebrity Cruises Halftime Show. Smokey Robinson and Martha Reeves did some neat singing.

And it was disclosed that Davis had been removed from the game suffering from a severe headache — a migraine.

The Packers kicked off to start the second half and the Broncos started from their 23. Davis was back. Elway handed Davis the ball on the first play and he fumbled. Tyrone Williams recovered at the 26 for Green Bay.

The Packers got to the 15 but twice were guilty of false starts on third down. They had to accept a 27-yard field goal by Ryan Longwell.

Barely three minutes into the second half of Super Bowl XXXII, the game was tied at 17-17. There had been a threat of another rout, but not by the Packers. And the threat had been eliminated.

It was a football game, pure and scintillating.

The Packers kicked off, and the Broncos started from their 28. Davis was back in the game full time. But Elway couldn't manage a first down. The teams again exchanged punts.

Midway through the third period, the Broncos started pinned back at their eight.

Elway was now in a fix similar to Favre's late in the first half.

The Broncos started with Elway's eight-yard pass to Sterling Sharpe, the loquacious tight end. Davis, feeling better, carried the ball on three successive plays for four, four and seven yards. The Broncos were whittling on the Packers' defense — Gilbert Brown, White, LeRoy Butler, Eugene Robinson.

After Davis' three runs, the Broncos were at their 31. It was first down. The Packers girded for Davis again. Elway faked the handoff and from the play action, passed up the right side to McCaffrey. McCaffrey advanced the ball to the Packers' 33. The gain was 36 yards.

And the Broncos kept moving. Davis for eight, Elway to McCaffrey for another nine, Davis again for three, then one. The Broncos were at the Packers' 12, third down-and-six. Elway took the ball and kept it and went to the right side. He scrambled his way to the four. An eight-yard gain. First down.

The Packers used one of their three time outs to regroup their defense. The time out would prove to be ill-advised.

The Broncos completed their 92-yard drive with Davis hitting the right side from the one. With 34 seconds left in the third quarter, the Broncos had a 24-17 lead over the reigning champions.

Denver quarterback John Elway calls out signals during Super Bowl XXXII. (Photo©James V. Biever)

The Broncos kicked off, and the Packers started from — they didn't start. Freeman fumbled the ball away. Tim McKyer recovered for the Broncos at the Packers' 22. Elway had a shot at another touchdown. He knew it and went for it — and a two-TD lead. Eugene Robinson intercepted the pass at the two.

It was a rescue job for Robinson. Favre immediately hit Freeman for a 27-yard gain to the 42 as the third period ended.

But the Broncos went into the fourth quarter with a lead few expected them to have. John Elway was 15 minutes from a cherished victory, the climax of a distinguished career that was lacking only an ultimate championship. Denver was one period away from ending the snickering and ridicule, the residue from four losses in four Super Bowls. The AFC was just a period from breaking a humiliating streak of 13 barren Super Bowls.

If only the Broncos could cling to their lead.

There was pride and ego involved now.

Bret Favre, the rollicking quarterback, vs. John Elway, the mountain man. It was Favre's ball.

And on the first play of the final period, he fired a pass downfield for Brooks. The ball fell to the turf. So did a yellow handkerchief. Pass interference against the Broncos' Darrien Gordon. The ball was moved 25 yards closer to Denver's goal line. It was spotted at the Broncos' 33.

Favre kept throwing, snapping the ball, whizzing it, as was his style. He passed three yards to Brooks, then 17 to Freeman. Favre had the Packers at the 13.

On the next play, he passed left and connected with Freeman for the touchdown. With better than 13½ minutes to play in regulation time, Super Bowl XXXII was tied at 24 points apiece.

No Super Bowl had ever played into overtime — sudden death.

The Packers kicked off and the Broncos started from their 22. Elway was unable to move them. The Broncos punted.

Green Bay started with advantageous field position at its 48. Favre had been able to move his offense longer distances on this afternoon. But his drive, too, now fizzled after one first-down pass to Levens. The Packers punted back to the Broncos.

Denver started from its 18. Elway moved the Broncos. Davis ran for 14 yards, then four and four, then three and three. Elway passed to Sharpe for 12, and the Broncos had crossed midfield to the Packers' 42. Three yards more, and this drive, also was aborted, after Elway threw two incompletions.

The suspense got stronger, Qualcomm louder, America's living rooms quieter.

The Packers started from their 11. The clock at the end of the stadium read 5:25.

Now it was time for the Packers to dig deep into their own history. Ancient and recent. Bart Starr's drive in the bitter Green Bay cold to get Vince Lombardi into his second Super Bowl. Favre's own brilliant accuracy in winning just a year before.

This time the Packers puttered. They self-destructed. An offensive holding penalty and a false start penalty, both charged against tackle Ross Verba, damaged the Packers. On third-down-and-11, back at his own 10, Favre passed incomplete. Craig Hentrich punted it away for the Packers.

The ball went 39 yards, and Gordon made the safe call, a fair catch.

The picture had changed once more. The Broncos had the ball one yard into the Packers' terrain. They had 3 minutes, 27 seconds left. It was too much time. They needed to move the ball only 15 yards, and they would be in Elam's field-goal range.

These were all factors as Shanahan and Holmgren plotted their strategies at the sidelines on opposite sides of the field.

There had been Super Bowls of this nature before. Super Bowl V, the comedy of errors, won by Baltimore over the Cowboys on a field goal with five seconds left. Super Bowl XIII when Terry Bradshaw and the Steelers managed to squeak past Roger Staubach and the Cowboys. Super Bowl XXIII when Joe Montana took the 49ers 92 yards against the clock to beat the Bengals. Super Bowl XXV when Jim Kelly took the Bills not quite close enough, and Scott Norwood's field-goal attempt just missed against the Giants.

They had all been colossal Super Bowls among all the duds through more than three decades.

But never before had there been the sentimental factor in the last minutes with the result still in deep suspense.

Now America watched John Elway . . . America from the gossipy White House across the continent to Hawaii. Now the world watched, across the Atlantic and across the Pacific, in Britain and across Europe, Africa, Australia, Asia. Citizens of 200 or so nations focused via their televisions on John Elway as he stepped up behind center Tom Nalen's butt with the ball at the Packers' 49-yard line.

No surprise. No trickery. No gimmick.

Elway took the snap and handed off the ball to Terrell Davis. Davis made a bare two years when the helmet and head that had contained the migraine was violently twisted. A flagrant face-mask penalty against Darius Holland. Fifteen yards.

The Broncos already had the yardage they needed to reach field-goal range. They were at the Packers' 32 with more than 2½ minutes left. Davis ran for a yard. The Broncos would have to shoot for a touchdown. They couldn't waste time fast enough. They would have to go for it, try to use up as much time as they could, and then return the ball to Favre.

Elway pitched a pass to Howard Griffith. Griffith got the ball to the eight for another first down.

The two-minute warning stopped the clock.

Davis now ran to the one, a seven-yard gain. But Sharpe was penalized for offensive holding. The Broncos were pushed back to their 18. The clock showed 1:54. Elway handed off to Davis again. Davis circled outside left end and broke into the open. He was headed for the orange cone at the goal line when Tyrone Williams shoved him out of bounds. The ball was at the one. The clock was stopped at 1:47.

The Broncos called time out. Then Elway huddled them. It was first down. Holmgren, at the Green Bay bench, calculated. "Second down," he thought. He quickly dispatched linebacker Bernardo Harris into the game, carrying a message.

On the next play, Terrell Davis cut over guard behind Nalen and Mark Schlereth and into the end zone for his third touchdown. The hole he ran through was immense. None of the Packers, surprisingly, put a hand on him. None even came close.

With 1:45 left, the Broncos had a 31-24 lead, and they were dancing on their sidelines.

But Bret Favre had one more shot — and much more time than the Broncos really wanted to give him. He had two time outs to use to stop the clock. The Packers had used up a precious time out, needlessly, in the third period.

The Broncos kicked off, and Freeman returned the ball 22 yards to the Packers' 30.

There was 1:39 on the clock. Favre passed to Levens, who reached the Broncos' 48 for a 22-yard gain.

There was 1:16 on the clock. Favre passed again to Levens. Romanowski made a huge tackle, stopping Levens for no gain. The Packers called their second time out. One left.

There was 1:11 on the clock. Favre passed again to Levens, who advanced the ball to the 35 for a 13-yard gain before he went out of bounds, stopped by John Mobley.

There was 1:04 on the clock, first down. Favre passed to Levens again, four yards to the 31, where Mobley made the tackle.

There was 0:42 on the clock, second down. Favre passed incomplete for Freeman.

There was 0:36 on the clock, third down. Favre passed incomplete for Brooks.

The Packers called their last time out. They worked out one last-ditch play. Then the Broncos called their second time out. They worked out their defense.

There was 0:36 on the clock, fourth down. Favre passed for Chmura over the middle. Mobley and Atwater went flying toward the ball, collided, they fell in pain to the grass.

So did the football.

The mighty, believed-to-be invincible Packers had been beaten. They had been beaten by the wild-card Denver Broncos.

There was 0:28 on the clock. John Elway took the snap and kneeled down at the 30-yard line.

Then he leaped in the air and raised both his arms in triumph.

Then he was mobbed by teammates, fans, cameramen, the world.

Upstairs, in the press boxes, nobody was heard to cheer. But a lot of hard-bitten, neutral journalists sort of felt good.

The Broncos had won a Super Bowl, 31-24. It took only five tries. The AFC had snapped the streak.

Down on the field, as the Denver mob swayed and cheered and hugged, somebody stuck a microphone into Elway's teeth.

"I'm going to Disneyland," said the Super Bowl champion — at last.

◆   ◆   ◆

Bill Romanowski did not spit. He threw a punch at Mark Chmura. The old-school tie came undone at the Super Bowl. Both had gone to Boston College.

On the field, Will McDonough, one of my eight newspaper colleagues who had covered each of the XXXII, pulled Romanowski to the side. McDonough worked all this time writing prose for the *Boston Globe*, but America got to know him for his TV gigs. He had the NBC mike on the field.

"How great they were, how great they were," Romanowski said of the advance notices for the Packers. "For two weeks we were saying how great they were.

"We said it so many times, I wanted to puke."

It was NBC's last hurrah with the NFL.

◆   ◆   ◆

It was dusk in San Diego. The NFL's corps of publicity people gradually guided the athletes, the victorious Broncos, the vanquished Packers. They had played a Super Bowl for the ages. Now they stood in special podiums, the Broncos on one side of the press tent on the Qualcomm Stadium parking lot, the Packers on the other side of the tent.

We jostled and shoved some more for positions around Elway and Shanahan and Terrell Davis — then scurried to the other side of the tent to listen to Holmgren and Favre.

◆   ◆   ◆

Hundreds gathered around Elway's area.

"You wonder if you're going to run out of years," Elway said. "But fortunately, I hung on, and Mike came in here and got it done for us."

It was an emotional moment.

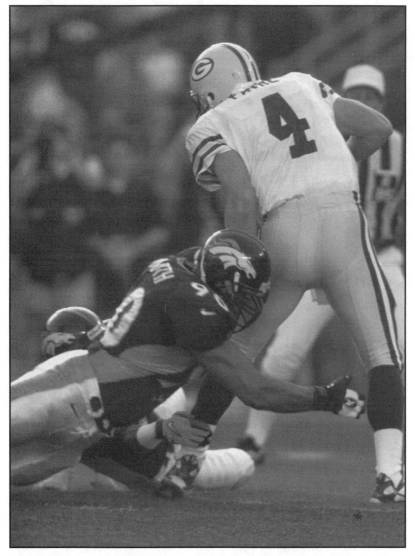

Despite being pressured throughout the game by Denver defenders, Green Bay quarterback Brett Favre nearly directed a last-minute drive that could have tied the game. (Photo©Vernon Biever)

"We hung in there, we made some plays when it counted, I'm very happy for John, the way he played," Shanahan said across the tent.

"For him to get the ring, I feel very proud not only for John, but for the whole city of Denver . . .

"The way John Elway plays exemplifies the way he is. He's going to throw his body on the line every time he plays. I watched him do that since the start of his career, so today was no different."

> *"You wonder if you're going to run out of years. But fortunately, I hung on, and Mike came in here and got it done for us."*
>
> *— John Elway*

Down the way, Davis, most valuable player of Super Bowl XXXII, told of what went on in his head.

"I got dinged," Davis told the curious media. "No, it was not a concussion. I don't think it was. I blinked out for a play and came to the sideline. My vision was blurred for a minute or so.

"I thought it was the onset of a migraine. I took some medication and the long halftime helped."

Moments later, Davis said he felt faint — could he please end the interview session, and go back to the locker room.

A mob surged back to Elway.

He talked about the final drive — scoring too soon, leaving Favre time to bring the Packers back.

"I was worried about it because we had first and goal on the one," Elway said. "I asked that when we got to the sideline. I said, 'Do you want to use some time or make them take a time out?'

"If we'd have known that we were going to get in there so easily, we probably would have wasted a little bit more time. We would have taken a knee or sneak or something . . ."

As it was, the gap opened, and Davis waltzed through it for the winner.

Already there were suspicions that the Packers had opened the gates, deliberately allowing Davis to score. They needed to conserve as much time as possible.

"I don't know because there wasn't anybody around," said Elway. "He walked in. It almost kind of looked that way that they let him in, so they could get the ball back."

A strange gambit for a Super Bowl finish.

The Migraine

◆　　◆　　◆

Two days after Super Bowl XXXII ended, and the nation had marveled at a football game, after Denver and the Broncos had partied, Mike Holmgren spoke to the press in Green Bay.

He confessed.

The message Holmgren sent to the Packers defense via Bernardo Harris with the ball on the one and 1:47 on the scoreboard was simple and to the point.

"We've got to let them score," Harris told his teammates.

"Let them score?" said Eugene Robinson, incredulous at his coach's call. Then Robinson looked at the clock and understood the logic.

The Packers must indeed allow Terrell Davis to score as part of a plan to save time and get back the ball.

Holmgren had a second confession. He had lost count of the downs.

"Second-and-goal from the one?" Holmgren said at his press conference when told it had been first down. "If that was the case, then we made a mistake. I thought what would happen if they used their time outs, kicked the field goal, we would have had about twenty-five seconds."

He wanted more time. He did not rue his decision.

"We made the decision," Holmgren said. "I wanted the ball back. At least we made it interesting. It was a strategy I felt was our only chance to win."

A week or so after the Broncos won the Super Bowl, Terrell Davis signed his first major product endorsement deal as a pitchman for a nasal-spray migraine medication, Migranal. He had used it on the sidelines and in the locker room at the half.

His first comment was: "If it wasn't for this product, I'm not sure I would have been able to finish the game."

Civilization marches on.

The Orange Hush

The ideal offensive lineman is anonymous. He sets up blocks for John Elway and Terrell Davis and gets his uniform very dirty, stained green and brown. Every once in a while, he will get his fingers caught in his blocking target's jersey, but that always is an accident. Never intentional, but that lousy ref, he dropped his yellow flag.

After a long gain, the offensive lineman might get a pat on the butt from the runner. But that's about all the praise he ever gets — and the silly sportswriters, they never interview offensive linemen anyway.

All of the above is part of the offensive lineman's lot in football. They are the grunge players, the ground forces, the troops in the trenches — all the battle cliches — and the idea is to remain unknown, anonymous.

But the idea is not to be deaf and dumb.

That is why the Broncos' offensive line caused such a commotion at the annual gabfest Media Day five days before Super Bowl XXXII.

Broncos offensive linemen Gary Zimmerman, Mark Schlereth, Tom Nalen, Brian Habib and Tony Jones had been deaf and dumb as far as we the media were concerned for two years. They had voluntarily shut up . . . well, it could have been at the urging of assistant head coach/offensive line coach Alex Gibbs. No journalist had heard a peep from any of these athletes during this period. Mum was the word. They ran silent, they ran deep.

The Denver media, with its flair for the original, nicknamed the Broncos' offensive line The Orange Hush.

Now, guys with zipped lips in sports are not uncommon. Steve Carlton refused to talk to the Philly baseball media and anybody else with a pen or camera or tape recorder. John Riggins played silent for two seasons. He rebuffed all interview efforts at Super Bowl XVII, except for a special-person press conference at which he showed up wearing war regalia. Then he was irreverent, funny, charming. And after he'd won the game for the Redskins, he spoke once more when President Reagan phoned congratulations:

"Ron's the president, but I'm the king."

The NFL could not tolerate such misbehavior . . . not on Media Day, not at the Super Bowl. Invoking what might be termed the Riggins Rule, Paul Tagliabue's minions ordered the Broncos' silent offensive linemen to speak out — or else.

The OR ELSE would be fines of $10,000 per player per silent day to be removed from their Super Bowl bonanza.

So when the Broncos' offensive linemen spoke, journalists listened. Scads of them.

"With a name like Zimmerman are you the only Jewish player in the NFL?" asked one of these media marvels to the Broncos' newly unzipped left tackle.

"I'm not Jewish," replied Zimmerman.

A journalistic breakthrough had been achieved, unmatched since another probing interviewing genius had asked Doug Williams at Super Bowl XXII the famed question: "Have you been a black quarterback all your life?"

It is the clinging presence of such wizards that makes lifelong football coaches such as Dr. Alex Gibbs shudder and desire to drop bowling balls on the invasive feet of the media.

"A confrontation," he said when forced to speak to the media at San Diego. He was, of course, surrounded by a huge contingent of the curious who did not know that he was fluent in English.

"They don't hire me or pay me to deal with you folks," Gibbs told the journalists. "And I don't just particularly enjoy it.

"This isn't what my job is . . . No this isn't helping me one bit. It helps you do your job, but it doesn't help my job. This isn't blocking Gilbert Brown. This isn't blocking Reggie White.

"I'm answering your questions, but I'm not giving you anything because I know what happens. Things get out of whack. More bad comes out of this than good.

"For every good story there are 10 bad ones. For every good comment there's six to eight misrepresented issues. It's not anybody's fault.

"It's the nature of the business."

Ah, the business . . .

Dr. Gibbs, according to his biography in the Broncos' media guide, earned three degrees — pre-law, masters in European history and doctorate in education. Nothing in economics or logic.

The NFL insists its Super Bowl performers speak — they may choose their own words — because television networks have agreed to pay $17.6 billion to display their football games. This was the theory that the NFL used in commanding the Broncos' offensive linemen to speak — and bear the journalistic fools at Super Bowl XXXII.

So there were all sorts of pithy quotes in the papers during Super Bowl week.

"My teammates think I'm a Kaczinski type," Zimmerman told the media when asked about his team nickname of The Unatackle.

He told the interrogators that he is a loner, a woodsman.

"I'm just more comfortable alone. I like to be by myself and hunt and fish."

Then there was Tony Jones, who believes he came back from the dead and now would be playing right tackle up against Reggie White in the Super Bowl.

He had played for the Cleveland Browns/Baltimore Ravens before joining the Broncos. Three years before this Super Bowl XXXII, Jones was in a Cleveland hospital for surgery on his elbow. He was given his anesthesia. His heart stopped. The doctors could not find a beat.

"I was dead," Jones told the Super Bowl writers. "I was a dead man. They had to bring me back . . .

"I really believe the Lord did that to me for a reason, and I truly believe He pulled me through. He was sending me a message that I had to change my life."

Mark Schlereth, the left guard told those around him about his 22 operations during his football career. He's had surgery to repair a herniated disc, his knees, his elbows, ankles and other assorted regions of his anatomy. But then he's a tough Alaskan who has played nine seasons in the NFL.

"What keeps bringing me back?" he said when asked.

"Nine parts stupidity, one part idiocy."

During a break in Gibbs' monologue, some journalist managed to hurl a football question at him.

What about Tom Nalen, the nervous center? After all, Nalen is so anonymous he gets to see most of the game upside-down and feel the familiar touch of John Elway.

"This guy's a throwback," said Gibbs, who of course preferred the linemen with broken teeth and wads of chewing tobacco in their cheeks back in the old days. "He's demanding of himself. He takes no shortcuts. He's the kind you want to hold up for high school players to emulate. He's a prototype. He knows that every day is important in terms of preparing to play. He's a special guy."

Now how do you twist up that commentary so as to create bad stories from good ones by a 10 to 1 ratio?

Part of the charm of the Denver offensive linemen was their Kangaroo court, the system in which players fine each other for transgressions.

Brian Habib, the right guard, was disclosed as the most demanding of the judges of the court. Zimmerman said Habib tried to fine backup lineman David Diaz-Infante when he skipped practice because his wife was in child birth. A few days later, Habib had to miss practice. He was incriminated by his own sense of justice.

Another time Habib was hit for a fine, supposedly $2,000, for trying to sneak onto a radio show.

"It turned into more of a game, a fun thing for us, than shunning the media," Habib told the media about the court when forced to break silence. "It was a camaraderie thing. Most of the time we're overlooked anyway."

And at Super Bowl XXXII they could have been overlooked again, these athletes of nearly 300 pounds who play behind face masks in football armor and are anonymous. The experts and analysts had figured the Packers' defensive linemen, Gilbert Brown, who approached 350 pounds, and Reggie White, would swarm over them.

The experts and analysts were wrong again.

The Broncos now not-quite-outspoken offensive linemen pushed Brown into exhaustion, held the great White to a single tackle. They opened the holes up front that enabled Terrell Davis to rush for his 157 yards and three touchdowns. They protected Elway when he dropped back and scrambled to pass.

And they were a major element in Denver's upset victory.

What motivated these guys?

Talk, said Gary Zimmerman in the postgame interviews. Talk.

"When you hear that for two weeks, it builds a fire under you," he said of all the talk about the prowess of the Packers. "We had to sit quiet and bite our tongues for two weeks and the last few days we've been having to suck it up and tell them how good they are.

"And we're pretty good ourselves."

Other books by Jerry Green

Year of the Tiger

Detroit Lions: Great Teams, GreatYears

Super Bowl Chronicles I

The Detroit Pistons: Capturing a Remarkable Era

Super Bowl Chronicles II

Quest for the Cup — The Detroit Red Wings' Unforgettable
Journey to the 1997 Stanley Cup (co-author)

Greatest Moments in Detroit Red Wings History (co-author)